THE AWESOME POWER of the LISTENING EAR

THE AWESOME POWER of the LISTENING EAR

by John Drakeford

WORD BOOKS   WACO, TEXAS

39455

First Printing—September 1967
Second Printing—January 1968
Third Printing—March 1969
Fourth Printing—September 1970
Fifth Printing—July 1971

CONTENTS

PART ONE
MASTERING THE ART OF LISTENING

PART TWO
ADVENTURES IN LISTENING

PART ONE

MASTERING
THE ART
OF LISTENING

CHAPTER 1

Decide If
It's Worth the Trouble

Why bother to listen?

If you are not convinced of the importance of listening don't fool with it. Of all the tasks you have ever undertaken, this will be the most frustrating, annoying, and aggravating if you are not altogether sold on its significance.

It may be you are too busy. Busyness is the most acceptable excuse anyone can offer in this activist society. Everybody is busy. So just say you are busy and forget all about it.

But what is the most important thing you do? If your work has to do with people it will probably involve listening. Most professional and semiprofessional people are faced with clients who come and consult for a variety of reasons, but, as much as anything else, need a listening ear.

The lawyer in the discussion of legal intricacies finds his client anxious to recount the background information. In divorce proceedings particularly the client is often in an emotional turmoil engendered by the events leading to the marital rupture and has a deep need to tell someone about it all.

A doctor seeing patients in his office frequently discovers them speaking through their bodies in "organ language."

It has been estimated that fifty per cent or more of the patients who come to a physician's office have nothing physically wrong with them. Faced with an obvious functional illness the doctor discusses it with the patient to discover he sometimes opens the lid of a seething cauldron of hostility, resentment, or self-pity. What should he do? Will he soothe it down with a good dose of tranquilizers, perhaps refer the patient to a psychiatrist, or listen with one eye on the clock, all the while haunted by a vision of the crowded waiting room?

The nurse working around sick people for long periods of time finds a growing closeness to them. As confidence grows they frequently want to talk. It has been suggested that the nurse not only helps the patient with the physical, but also the "psychological" bath. There is an interiorized soiling, and in the weakness and uncertainties of sickness when a patient may interpret illness as a punishment, he is ready to bare his soul, so he apprehensively gestures for the nurse's listening ear.

The concerns of America's women are nowhere more graphically illustrated than in the tremendous number of beauty shops dotted across the country and dedicated to helping turn out the well-groomed American woman. With great regularity milady hurries to her appointment to be primped, prodded, and pampered as she has her hair shampooed, frosted, rinsed, set or cut, fingers manicured, toenails pedicured, face worked over, eyebrows shaped, or eyelashes dyed. These attentions apparently help the jaded ego as is evidenced by the frequently heard statement, "I feel so much better after I have been to the beauty shop."

This unlikely institution, with graduates from such esoteric academies of higher learning as Isbell's University of Beauty Culture, may be the new frontier of psychotherapy, unwittingly demonstrating that beauty is *not* skin deep. Women spending hours with their operators pour out stories of trouble with the children, the struggle of money management, thoughtless husbands, and the complexities of a modern woman's life. Details of the most personal aspects of husband-wife relations are intimate enough to make the hair dryer blow a fuse.

All of this comes because of the listening ear of a beauty operator. Sometimes with a limited formal education, but with wide experience of life and senses not too easily shocked, she is well remunerated for her work. Before you make any comments on her rate of pay, remember unwitting psychotherapeutic skills which may justify payment equivalent to the psychiatrist, plus the fact that she need have no professional scruples about accepting a tip. Madam's feeling of well-being as she leaves the salon may in no small measure be related to the operator's capacity to listen.

All of these people are busy with their own particular work, and none are trained to listen as is the minister, the man who is called to the "cure of souls." Surely he will be waiting for the person with the weary heart. But will he listen?

In her own inimitable and sympathetic way Taylor Caldwell has come to the defense of ministers who fail to listen. She says, "Our pastors would listen—if we gave them the time to listen to us. But we have burdened them with tasks which should be our own. We have demanded not only that they be our shepherds but that they take our trivialities, our social aspirations, the 'fun' of our children, on their weary backs. We have demanded that they be expert business men, politicians, accountants, playmates, community directors, 'good fellows,' judges, lawyers, and settlers of local quarrels. We have given to them little time for listening, and we do not listen to them, either. We must offer them concrete help and assume our own responsibilities. We forget that they are men also, frequently very tired, always unappreciated, sometimes disheartened, quite often appalled, worried, anxious, lonely, grieved. They are not supermen without human agony and human longing. Heedlessly, we neglect them—unless we wish them to serve us in material ways, when their ways should be exclusively God's. We demand of them what we would not dare to demand of anyone else, even ourselves. We give them no time to listen when to have someone listen, without hurry, without the click of a clock, is the direst need of our spirits."[1]

The authoress is kind. Of all professional people the minister is least bound by a schedule. He punches no clock and has no supervisor checking on his arrival and departure.

Rather unfortunately, he has not always been adequately prepared for his task. Much of his theological training has aimed at intellectualizing theological concepts. In his practical preparation a goodly portion of the time has been spent teaching him to project himself and express his thoughts with clarity and persuasiveness. But to listen! He's much too busy with the mechanics of church life to spend time at that.

In actual fact the biggest majority of his church members would be delighted if they knew their pastor spent more time listening to people. With a little effort he could organize his time to make provision for such a vital ministry.

I chanced to pick up a book in the home of a friend. The book was called *The Listener* and was inscribed:

> To my Preacher
> with deepest gratitude for being
> my "listener" in my hour of need.

Reading the statement, I felt not a little envious of this minister and the way he was seen by his parishioner. It was one of the highest compliments any church member could pay a pastor.

Consider The Possibilities

Sit down and remind yourself about the important place of listening in life. Preview the following facts which will be presented in Part Two of this book.

- Poor listening is responsible for a tremendous waste in education, industry, and many other areas of life.
- Any capable democratic leader can immeasurably improve his effectiveness by cultivating a listening ear.
- Time spent in listening plays a vital part in building good relationships with people.
- Marriages that are sick can often be strengthened when husbands and wives will learn to listen to each other.
- As we listen to people we help them break out of their skin-enclosed isolation and enter into the community of experience and discover their potential.
- All forms of psychotherapy emphasize that listening is probably the most simple and effective single technique for helping troubled people.

Surely a skill that would accomplish these objectives is worthy of acquisition.

Listening is an art. Have this in mind if you aspire to be a competent listener. To the casual observer it may seem that the artist's effortless achievements are simply native gifts. However, while artists are undoubtedly born not made, they are certainly not born made. Years of observation, study, and hard work lie behind the smooth performance. Laborious hours have polished the roughhewn crystalline carbon of capacity until it shines in all its multifaceted diamond brilliance.

There is no easy pathway to the goal of effective listening. Once we accept the proposition that listening is an art, we must realize that it may require as much time, effort, and perseverance as painting, ballet, music, or any other of the art forms.

Convinced? Make up your mind to let nothing keep you from mastering this art. Consider how valuable this skill will be in all that you do. Resolutely discipline yourself and launch into an enterprise that may revolutionize your life.

The next nine chapters of this book present a plan for developing latent listening skills by taking the following steps:

- Work on your listening inertia.
- Concentrate on the speaker—it's indispensable.
- Demonstrate! It may be the only way.
- Listen without ears.
- Listen for the sound of silence.
- Consider your listener's perspective.
- Beware of three traps of listening.
- Cultivate the skill of reply.
- Ask a question—but do it carefully.

Work at it systematically and methodically.

1. Read the next nine chapters through in one sitting.
2. Go back and concentrate on the chapters that were not clear in the first reading.
3. Proceed to Part Two and discover the possibilities of applying listening skills.
4. Practice, practice, practice.

CHAPTER 2

Work On
Your Listening Inertia

Any serious student of listening must commence by clarifying the similarities and contrasts between the two human functions of hearing and listening. To the uninitiated the two expressions may appear to refer to the same activity, but in actual fact there is a world of difference between the two.

Hearing is a word used to describe the physiological sensory processes by which auditory impressions are received by the ears and transmitted to the brain. *Listening*, on the other hand, refers to a more complex psychological procedure involving interpreting and understanding the significance of the sensory experience.

In his book *Witness*, Whittaker Chambers tells of an experience which led him to abandon his atheism and ultimately his membership in the Communist party. Standing one night and looking down at his sleeping daughter he was overwhelmed by the beautifully intricate formation of her ear. He finally concluded, "No, these ears were not created by chance. . . ."[1]

Any inquirer who pauses to consider the subject of human auscultation—the act of listening—must not only be impressed by the shape of the ear but also the whole complex functioning of human audition.

17

The mechanism of the ear itself is made up of three parts: the external ear, the middle ear, and the inner ear. All play a peculiar role in the hearing process.

The outer ear includes the delicately sculptured and arranged auricle, a sound trumpet which catches the sound waves and guides them into a passage of about one-and-a-half inches called the auditory channel. The outer third of this channel is lined with tiny, wax-producing glands and fine hairs that constitute a gentle but effective barrier to discourage inquisitive insects and keep out foreign bodies.

Separating the outer ear from the middle ear is the eardrum, or tympanic membrane, a thin sheet of tissue about a quarter of an inch in diameter. Sound waves vibrate the eardrum which in turn touches the first of three moveable bones closely linked to each other. Called the auditory ossicles, these bones are of unusual shapes which have given them their picturesque names. Attached to the eardrum is the malleus or hammer, which rests against the incus or anvil that in turn impinges on the stapes or stirrup.

To the hammer, anvil, and stirrup is added a snail-shaped mechanism, the cochlea, known more popularly as the inner ear. Sound vibrations move the stapes or stirrup in and out of an oval window in the cochlea disturbing the liquid called perilymph which vibrates some of the twenty-four thousand fibers of the basilar membrane and stimulates the attached nerves.

From this "organ of corti," as it is called, the neural current flows through the auditory nerve to the temporal lobe of the brain. The cortex or "bark" of the brain is grey in color and covered with a tremendous number of neurons which are interrelated and provide a fantastic number of circuits that can be hooked up, allowing the neural current to be routed in a great variety of directions.

The whole operation of a sound wave hitting the ear, and being transmitted to the brain, takes place with lightning speed. The brain itself is programed by years of experience and conditioning to handle the auditory impressions with which it is fed. Like a busy executive's efficient secretary who sorts out the correspondence, keeping only the most important for his personal perusal, some sounds are summarily rejected, while others have the total attention focused on them.

This selective process carried on by the brain is the main distinction and difference between hearing and listening. From the total number of our auditory impressions we choose a small select number upon which to focus our attention. As the sounds come to us we *hear;* when we apply ourselves to their meaning and significance we *listen.*

Not unlike the ground crews of jet airlines who carefully position ear guards for protection against the earsplitting sounds of the whining engines, modern man has had to develop a self-protective mechanism to defend himself from the constant acoustical bombardment of twentieth-century living. Most humans are engaged in a lifelong process of gradually building up their own personal internal ear plugs and training themselves to ignore certain sounds.

I once went to live in a house located near a railroad track. For the first few nights every passing train disturbed my sleep. As time went on, I grew to be less and less aware of the nearby activity. One evening a visitor inquired if the passing trains bothered me. I replied, "What trains?" My internal squelching mechanism had taken over so that I no longer listened to the railroad noises.

There is obviously wisdom in the natural tendency we have *not to listen.* The mechanism protects us in so many ways. But it also does us a disservice, because it causes us to miss many of the things to which we should listen. A really observant person has to work hard to overcome what we might call his natural "listening inertia."

Leftover Time

One of the problems with listening is that we have time to spare. While some speakers may verbalize at about 125 words a minute, most of us can think at about four times that speed. As the speaker presents his ideas we can easily move along and keep up with him. It is so simple that we have time on our hands so we can occasionally dart ahead or go on a side excursion. These side excursions are particularly damaging and lead to our downfall as listeners.

As you sit in an audience listening to a speaker you may move along with him for a short period. Then a picture of the office flashes onto the screen of your mind and you see the work awaiting your attention. So you take a mental trip back to your place of toil, look over your correspondence, check up on your coffee-drinking secretary, and then rejoin the speaker.

A little later in the discourse the golf course begins to beckon, and off you go. You bask in the warm sun, admire the condition of the greens, see the old cronies. Mentally you visualize the beautiful drive, the flawless putt, your opponent's dismay, and the concluding moment of triumph.

But on one of these side journeys you stay away too long and when you return it is to discover the speaker has gotten so far ahead that there is no chance of catching him now. So you sink into a passive resignation to your horrible fate, put a fixed look on your face, and hope the speaker will soon tire and quit.

Capturing the Balloons

The process of a speaker, addressing an audience has been envisaged in a number of different ways. One older method was to imagine that each listener had a funnel-like appurtenance fitting on the top of his head. The speaker carried his store of ideas like water in a bucket and conceived his chief task as pouring ideas into the funnel-heads of his auditors.

Because of his distance from the funnel-heads, the speaker was forced to resort to tossing out his buckets of ideas, hoping his aim would be good enough to slosh at least some tiny droplets into the funnels. Thus the listener was a passive recipient, and the number of ideas he received depended mainly on the throwing ability of the speaker.

A much more productive way for the lecturer to see his audience would be to change them from funnel-heads to something more like women sitting in the beauty shop with roller-covered heads. These roller-like contraptions are bumps of knowledge complete with tie-on strings. They are the concepts already possessed by the listeners and the protruding strings are waiting for familiar thoughts and concepts to be attached.

The communicator on the platform is launching balloons inscribed with messages printed in large letters. Each of his idea-balloons trails a long string, making it a simple matter for the listener to grasp it as it passes by.

While much of the speaker's ability lies in his capacity to adapt his idea-balloons so that they match the more obvious tie-down spots on his auditors' heads, the listener is no quiescent squeezed-out sponge. The listener's activity is just as important in communication as the speaker's skill.

A prospective listener sits in an audience. The speaker launches his balloons and sends them floating across the room trailing their strings. As they sail toward the listener he is faced with the responsibility for some action and has at least three alternatives.

He may be bodily present but only partly conscious. In his sleepy mistiness he is only vaguely aware of his surroundings. The idea-balloons drift lazily by. For all he knows they may only be spots before his eyes, so he pays them scant attention, content to relax in the twilight zone of inattentive half-sleep.

Or perhaps the balloons look a little unusual, and for a brief moment he toys with the possibility of closer acquaintance. But they are a trifle strange and bear little relationship to the bumps on his head. After a casual glance he lets them drift on their way.

A third possibility is that the listener may examine the balloons very closely. He notes even the slightest resemblances to the stringed bumps on his head. As the balloons come closer he becomes more intent. He is enthralled with the potential of these concepts. He searches his mind for associated ideas. He reaches out, takes a firm grip on the strings, and begins to tie them securely to his previous knowledge. These new ideas are now his.

It is this third attitude that is a must for the listener.

Try an exercise in listening. Listen to someone talking, a political or after-dinner speech, a sermon, or a troubled person who wants to tell his story. Enter actively into the experience in the following ways:

- Start with a determination to overcome your listening inertia. Like the Naval message give yourself a strong and certain "Now hear this."
- Examine the facts as they are presented and try to determine if they are accurate or are just being presented to prove a point or used to bolster a case.

- Look for a message beyond the words. The changing tones and fluctuating facial expressions, gestures and bodily movements all carry a message.
- The speaker may have something to say that you need to hear. Decide not to let your prejudice block you from appreciating and evaluating the message.
- Fight distractions. Refuse to be lured away by your curiosity. Reject the incidentals, interruptions, and any peripheral activity.
- Try to anticipate where the speaker is going. Scout on ahead. If he goes on another trail, retrace your steps and rejoin him.
- Focus your attention on the theme or main message. See how other material bolsters this basic idea.
- Make mental summaries periodically so that you know where you've been and have a launching pad for what follows.
- Underline the illustrations and examples. They will become easily remembered reference points.

This exercise may be valuable in many ways. What you listen to will become much more interesting and rewarding. You may even discover another bonus.

When I first became interested in listening I began to research the books I felt would contain the information I needed. Naturally I turned to the extensive literature of psychology, clinical psychology, and psychotherapy, but there was little to be found. Then I unearthed an unexpected wealth of information. It was in the books on speech.

The authorities in the field of speech early realized that to become a good speaker the student must first of all learn to listen. As you learn to listen, you may find you have unwittingly grasped the principles of good expression and finished up as a speaker to whom other people will want to listen.

CHAPTER 3

Concentrate on the
Speaker—It's Indispensable

One of the popular stories of hospital life tells of two doctors meeting in the hospital corridor. The orthopedic surgeon is commiserating with the psychiatrist, "I don't know how you can spend all your day listening to people . . ."

The psychiatrist replies, "Who listens?"

Who indeed?

Listening is really hard work. It calls for the expenditure of effort in concentrating to defeat our listening inertia. Listening cannot be carried on as a part-time activity; it must be entered into with all the vigor we can muster.

Returning from the rural area where I was pastoring my first church, I thrilled with excitement at the prospect of seeing my former pastor. I had so many stories to tell him. Entering his office, we shook hands and then sat down as I started to recount my story.

Bubbling over with enthusiasm, I poured out my tale. To my amazement my friend didn't even look me in the eyes. He straightened up his desk top, pushed sundry pens and pencils into place, leaned over to pull out a drawer, and moved around its contents. Now and then he half glanced my way.

My story slowed down. Its importance gradually diminished and finally I limped to a conclusion, made a lame excuse, and left his office. It was one of the most disappointing encounters of my life.

In a later frank interview the man told me he had really been interested in what I had to tell but just wanted to make the most use of his time, hence his tidying-up effort. He might have finished with a neat desk but he had ruined a relationship. He had not learned to listen.

During World War II Australian women industriously knitted socks for soldiers. At any and every meeting they considered it their patriotic duty to keep the knitting needles constantly on the move. They undoubtedly were the most difficult of all groups to which to speak. With clicking needles and vacant faces that told the story of mental calculations of stitches and patterns, there was absolutely no inspiration for a speaker.

And make no mistake about it. A listening audience is more than half the secret of any successful speech. A group with any sizable number of people who refuse to take an interest in the speaker can transform an eloquent orator into a halting, hesitant, dry-as-dust talker.

Since writing the foregoing I stumbled upon a passage from the writings of Charles Hadden Spurgeon. Sometimes called the "Prince of Preachers," Spurgeon was one of the adornments of the Victorian era. Five or six thousand people jammed his church, morning and evening, every Sunday for years. With no musical instruments or complex educational organization in his church, the sermon was the main feature of his church service. This brilliant orator had a preaching ability rarely heard before or since.

Among other activities he organized a theological college for training of ministers. His lectures to these students are gems of wit and wisdom. In one of the lectures on the subject

of "attention" he voiced his reaction to inattentive auditors:
". . . they are not in the habit of attending. They attend
the chapel but do not attend to the preacher. They are ac-
customed to look around at every one who enters the place,
and they come in at all times, sometimes with much stamp-
ing, squeaking of boots, and banging of doors. I was preaching once to a people who continually looked around, and
I adopted the expedient of saying, 'Now, friends, as it is so
very interesting to you to know who comes in, and it dis-
turbs me so very much for you to look around, I will, if you
like, describe each one as he comes in, so that you may sit
and look at me, and keep up at least a show of decency.' I
described one gentleman who came in, who happened to be
a friend whom I could depict without offense, as 'a very
respectable gentleman who had just taken his hat off,' and
so on; and after that one attempt I found it was not necessary to describe any more, because they felt shocked at what
I was doing, and I assured them that I was much more
shocked that they should render it necessary for me to reduce
their conduct to such absurdity. It cured them for the time
being, and I hope for ever, much to their pastor's joy."[1]

The distressed preacher went on to describe how people
who were not listening affected him. He maintained that
he wanted all eyes fixed on him and all ears opened to him.
He added, "To me it is an annoyance if even a blind man
does not look me in the face."[2]

Dr. Ralph D. Nichols of the University of Minnesota
has written with clarity about the importance of listening.
He tells of going to a high school commencement in which,
from the speaker's point of view, everything went wrong.
One child began to cry; then another swelled the chorus.
A small boy galloped up and down the aisle, and he was
joined by another who chased him. Nichols had the sinking

feeling which only a public speaker knows, when he realizes he has lost his audience.

The speaker tried every trick of his trade. He spoke louder, told a funny story, walked around the stage, peered intently and disapprovingly at the area of disturbance. But all was to no avail.

Then he tried his last desperate trick. He found one good listener. An elderly gentleman in the first row was looking up smiling and nodding his head. Concentrating all his attention on this one listener, the speaker gradually salvaged the situation and the speech was saved.

During the refreshment period that followed, Nichols asked the school superintendent to introduce him to the old gentleman who sat on the front row.

"Well, yes, I'll try to introduce you," said the superintendent, "but it may be difficult. You see, the old fellow is stone deaf."[3]

Unable to hear, the deaf man had saved the day by concentrating his attention on the speaker.

If you are going to be an effective listener, you must give the speaker your undivided attention. It is his moment and every aspect of your demeanor must say, "Come on. Let's have it. You're in the center of the stage in my thinking."

The good listener doesn't do a lot of things. He cannot lean back in his chair with eyes half closed as if he were taking his afternoon nap—none of those furtive looks as if mentally cataloging the books on his shelves. He doesn't steal glances at his watch with the inference, "Time is up; you've been here long enough." No doodling on a pad as though preparing an entry for a museum of modern art.

The good listener is relaxed. The telephone is cared for, his secretary warned against interruptions. He leans slightly toward the speaker, his eyes focused on him, not in a staring match, but in a coaxing, interested manner. Every aspect of the listening one says, "Tell me more."

Watch your speaker blossom as he becomes aware of the situation. See the way in which he drops his defenses, note the growing confidence in his bearing. Far too long he has been on the receiving end, and now he has a chance to express his ideas.

The good listener is a man with a mission. Every power of body and mind is focused on the listening task.

CHAPTER 4

Demonstrate!
It May Be the Only Way

In the years of the Great Depression I tried my hand at selling—door to door selling. Anxious to succeed in this difficult task, I drank in every word that fell from the sales manager's lips. In his lectures he made it sound so easy as he faced hypothetical difficulties and casually vanquished them. Despite the enthusiastic presentation, however, I felt far from confident, and told the lecturer of my fears.

Trying to bolster our courage, the manager took two of us out on the road. We stopped near a residence. He led the way, and we sheepishly followed. With cool aplomb he knocked on the door, and, as it was opened, courteously introduced himself and proceeded with his sales pitch. The housewife was impressed, responded, and made a purchase.

That one example of successful selling did more to teach me, and give me confidence, than twenty lectures could have. The demonstration gave a concrete form to the ideas which were previously so nebulous.

This same principle may be applied to the task of encouraging people to talk. It frequently happens that the very individuals who most need to verbalize have the least ability to express themselves. This may have been an important factor in bringing on their trouble. The situation calls for some type of pump-priming technique to help the subject "get it off his chest."

Probably the most objectionable aspect of the older *directive* methods of counseling was that the counselor did all the talking. He generally sat behind a desk, an all-wise Buddha. As soon as possible he broke in, like a father lecturing his erring child, to tell his counselee how he should act. The counselee was on the receiving end and given little opportunity to express himself.

Wider experience led to the formulation of the so-called *nondirective* techniques in counseling. The main skill of the counselor lay in encouraging his counselee to talk. He listened, tried not to interrupt, and bent every effort to encouraging the flow of conversation by the use of short monosyllabic responses. Unfortunately, his method was severely limited. Some people weren't able to express themselves while others just couldn't catch on to what it was all about.

Counseling has travelled two different types of streets. There were the one-way theories—directive from counselor to counselee and nondirective from counselee to counselor. Now has come a new two-way process. It is a concrete example of the much talked about but highly theoretical idea of dialogue. At the heart of this counseling theory is a process of give and take between two responsible beings. Neither is superior to the other, and they become engaged in a dialogue by which they enter into each other's experiences.

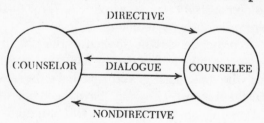

A group of researchers in the field of psychotherapy has provided a framework within which the technique of dialogue can be utilized. The method has been intuitively used by people across the years but seldom approved by psychotherapists. Trainee counselors have been repeatedly warned to avoid talking about themselves. As we will later see, this is a fairly good general rule, but there is evidence to show that there are some significant exceptions.

This new therapy, known as Integrity Therapy, emphasizes the place of values in human experience and contends that "disturbed" people are frequently in that condition because they have transgressed their values and become secretive about their failures. Therapy involves becoming "open," involvement in group interaction, and learning a new style of life.

Although it is a group method, Integrity Therapy commences with a personal one-to-one intake interview. The central feature of this initial interview is the moment when, after hearing the distressed person's story, the therapist "models the role."

The best way to teach a skill is to demonstrate it. An old adage says, "Those who can, do; those who can't, teach." The very best teachers are obviously those who both *teach* and *do*. The example they show by their actions reinforces the theories they have advanced, and this is exactly what is done in "modeling the role."

An individual under stress lives in a prison house, cut off and isolated from his fellows. Even when he plucks up courage to talk with someone about his difficulties he wonders if they will understand. The Integrity Therapist tells him there is no need to remain in isolation. He himself has been in trouble because of his own irresponsibility. The troubled person is no longer alone. Someone who understands his difficulty is waiting to help. He can safely speak. Let us look in on an Integrity Therapist at work.

Sydney Williams: I have not been feeling well. Every now and then there sweeps over me this sense that something terrible is going to happen. Life seems empty. I wake up miserable and spend the day longing for night when I can take a pill and drop off to sleep.

Reverend Harris: How long have you been experiencing this feeling?

Sydney Williams: It first seemed to come on me after a crisis where I work. I was anticipating a promotion. The manager had just about promised me the job. He didn't actually say it but he had hinted a few times.

Then there was this young guy who was a real eager beaver. I helped him get started when he first came to work for us. Well, the boss gave him the job. Oh boy, did it really tear me up. I went home that night and just sat. I didn't want to talk to Kay and the kids, just sat.

Reverend Harris: You feel missing this promotion has made you anxious.

Sydney Williams: Yes, it was just a big disappointment. I thought I'd get over it, but it's been a month now and I'm still depressed.

Reverend Harris: This is certainly very strange. You know, I had a terrible depression at one time and I felt somewhat the same way as you describe.

Sydney Williams: You did! What happened to you?

Reverend Harris: What *happened* to me? That's what I thought at first, but later I came to see it wasn't so much what had happened to me as what I had done.

Sydney Williams: Done?

Reverend Harris: It was a silly thing in many ways. I learned to play golf and really got the bug. I played every day. Both my wife and my secretary covered up for me. I missed sick calls, didn't prepare my sermons, ducked committee meetings. I guess you could say I was a golf bum.

Oh, I had it all rationalized. I was looking after my health.

Someone had to minister to these people on the golf course and so on. Then I started to spend time at the nineteenth hole.

One day one of my deacons took me on one side and suggested I had better not spend so much time at the country club. People were beginning to talk about it.

I was filled with righteous indignation. Just like those narrow-minded bigots to pick on my golf. I became depressed, just wanted to sit in a corner and feel sorry for myself. I felt these people had brought on my condition.

Then it began to dawn on me. My depression was no mystery. I had been misbehaving, acting irresponsibly, and I deserved to feel the way I did.

Is there any possibility that you may have behaved irresponsibly and your depressed feelings may come from poor actions?

A long period of silence follows.

Sydney Williams: You surely hit me, preacher. I'd never thought of you as ducking your responsibility. As a matter of fact, I guess I really got all I deserved. I have been much too friendly with my secretary. The boss hinted to me a couple of times that it didn't look too good, but I reckoned it was none of his business.

Let me tell you what has happened. . . .

The minister had undertaken a difficult task. He had modelled the role. It was a calculated risk but also a gesture of openness which touched Williams' heart and made it easier for him to talk.

Demonstrate! It may be the only way.

CHAPTER 5

Listening Without Ears

The strangest things happen to people when they get behind the wheel of an automobile. I am thinking of Mrs. McLean, a sweet, sedate, middle-aged woman who presides over her household with efficiency, participates in P.T.A., and plays a responsible role in civic affairs. She is the personification of middle-class virtue and a pillar of strength in her church.

But let her take a trip down the highway in her Oldsmobile and a remarkable metamorphosis takes place. And it is not for the better. She is soon muttering under her breath about the ineptitude of other drivers. At the intersection light she refuses to be beaten and steps on the throttle with all the enthusiasm of a teenage dragster.

When she gets onto the turnpike it might seem to the observer that she is participating in the qualifying trials for the Indianapolis 500. Mrs. McLean in her Oldsmobile can hold her own against the most uninhibited college sophomore.

One trip with her to a church convention left the minister's wife completely terrified by, and puzzled about, Mrs. McLean, and inwardly vowing she would never again risk her life in such a hazardous venture.

34

Is the automobile the last outpost of individuality? In other forms of transportation—bus, train, or plane—travelling is a shared enterprise; but not so with the automobile. At a social function a man entered the room and said, "Come on now, admit it. What tightwad family all came in one car?"

When the Russian leader, Nikita Khrushchev, visited the United States and watched the cars streaming down a San Francisco freeway, his critical comment was that so many cars with just one driver was an awful waste of transportation.

The car may be the logical descendent of the cowboy's bronco. Like that noble beast it apparently ideally carries one person. Any additional passengers are only taken under exceptional circumstances. The automobile driver is cut off from his fellows and out of communication with them.

This lack of communication may be the most important single factor in the tragedy of highway death toll. One answer to the situation could be for motorists to develop new and better ways of communicating with each other.

A recent writer tells of travelling with a particularly skillful driver, Mr. Harold L. Smith, who has developed the "Smith System of No Accident Driving."[1] Easily the most important aspect of this technique is the manner in which a driver may communicate his intentions to other drivers without uttering a single word.

The technique involves drifting gradually in the direction of an anticipated turn, gently tapping the brakes of the car, nodding the head to show a following driver you realize he wants to pass, flashing headlights and brakelights to warn of an emergency, sounding the horn in a friendly, beeping manner. To get into a lane of slow moving traffic it is suggested: Choose one driver in the oncoming line and look at him. And in that look—*ask!* Says Smith: Try to get eye-to-eye contact. Give him a quick, friendly wave of the hand. And add a big, friendly smile—just in case. With such "talk," Smith says, you rarely have to ask more than two drivers.[2]

The observer told of Smith held behind a car after the signal had changed. He gave his horn a nudge. It came out louder than he anticipated. The other driver glared at Smith. "At the next traffic light we pulled up alongside the driver. Smith's hand came up in a cheerful little salute. As clearly as if he'd spoken, Smith was saying, Sorry, friend, those things 'happen.'

"The other driver began to smile. And suddenly he was waggling back, a little salute which clearly said, 'That's all right, forget it.'"[3]

It doesn't require much imagination to see how this form of communication without words could do such a lot to help our shameful highway situation.

The commodities market in Chicago is the largest in the world, and through its transactions millions of bushels of wheat, corn, oats, rye, and soybeans are bought and sold. Some of these crops have not yet been harvested, others are even unplanted. Commodities are sold in 5000-bushel lots and the transactions are carried out by hand signals. An observer describes the scene, ". . . palm up and in when the broker is buying and up and out when he is selling. Fingers are held horizontally and manipulated to indicate prices offered or asked."[4] Intricate negotiations involving great quantities of produce and large sums of money are expertly carried on without words.

The Australian poet, Banjo Patterson, has a narrative poem in which he recounts the experience of a country boy who came to the big city wearing a beard. Feeling somewhat out of place, he decided to visit the barber's shop and have his whiskers shaved.

The barber, a typical city slicker, had a group of idlers who lounged around the seats in his establishment. As the country boy entered the shop the barber decided to play a joke on him. The poet describes the way the barber conveyed his message to the idlers.

> To them the barber cast a wink,
> One dexter eyelid shut,
> "I'll make this blooming yokel think
> His blooming throat is cut."[5]

A wink from the barber told the story with clarity and conciseness.

Watch an interpreter to the deaf carrying on his work. The silent flying fingers are telling their message. Even music is translated into action and conveyed to the non-hearing listeners.

"Standing Room Only for Silence" was the title of an article reporting on an entertainer who never spoke a single word. He is the Frenchman, Marcel Marceau, who, though he speaks four languages, prefers to appear on the stage without saying a single word and tell his stories by the actions of his body and expressions of his face. His own explanation of his success is that people desperately want to be communicated with, and his pantomimicry breaks through language barriers and provides a medium of universal communication.

Although pantomime is comparatively new in the United States, Marceau tells his interviewers it is one of the best known techniques of entertainment. The actors of the silent screen were past masters of this method, as you may readily realize while watching the old movies of Charlie Chaplin, Buster Keaton, Laurel and Hardy, and many other of the old time actors. The gesture, smile, forlorn look, pathetic walk all tell their own story.

When Marceau first came to the United States from France the agents saw no possibilities for his acts. One verdict was: "No sex, no scenery and he doesn't say a word? It will never be commercial."[6] Yet so popular did his acts become that he has been in constant demand in the theater and on television. His techniques of communication without words are so effective that the people in the audience will sometimes shout out a response to the scene he portrays.

Speakers and actors have been particularly aware of the effectiveness of this method of conveying their messages. Psychologists use the term "nonverbal communication" to describe these ways of expressing ideas or emotions.

The greeting customs of many people give mute evidence of the truthfulness of the saying that actions speak louder than words. I have a Hungarian friend who, though a humble and kind person, greets me with such a clicking of heels that I feel the appropriate response would be to return a military salute or cringe in subjection. He contrasts with an Indian I sometimes encounter who makes me feel as if I have been suddenly deified as he obsequiously puts his palms together and bows his head.

Touch conveys a message. The Russian bear hug may represent the Marxian dialectic of warmth and warning. Anglo-Saxon handshakes convey messages all the way from the enthusiastic bone cruncher to the extremity dropped like a dead fish into the greeter's waiting hand.

A kiss has an intimacy all its own. It varies from the child's grimace to the maiden aunt's flamboyant embrace, the therapeutic maternal "kiss-it-better" effort to the complex and prolonged expression of love.

A man passes on a message by the way he smokes,

straightens his tie, toys with his glasses, adjusts his belt, bites his fingernails, crosses his legs, or squints his eye.

I once sat with a counselor as a woman poured out a sordid story. The counselor listened and uttered never a word as she recounted her experiences. At last she paused, then asked, "What do you think of that?"

The counselor looked at her for a moment, then wrinkled his nose. That wrinkled nose said far more than any words he could say.

We are laboring under a grave misapprehension when we imagine listening is carried on with the ears alone. While we hear with our ears the complete listening process involves using the total body. We can listen with our eyes, hands, arms, feet, head. The whole body becomes involved in the process.

Take time to learn "nonverbal communication." Try out different ways of doing it: the nod of the head, movement of the body, gesture of the hand, wrinkled nose or forehead. These and a dozen bodily movements encourage a speaker and help make the listener more effective.

CHAPTER 6

Listen for
the Sound of Silence

The Chinese girl who sat on the front row of classroom seats was the type of student for whom every teacher longs. She looked up with eager eye, periodically writing in her notebook with great rapidity, giving the impression that she must catch every pearl of wisdom as it fell from the lecturer's lips.

As I remember it, there was only one occasion when she did not give her wholehearted assent to everything I said. In fact, she let out a startled cry that temporarily disorganized the class.

While discussing the listening process I had used Dominick Barbara's phrase and was exhorting my students to "listen for the sound of silence."

My favorite Oriental student exclaimed in painful dismay, "Sound of silence! How can silence have a sound?"

The expression which upset a girl already puzzled by the intricacies of the English language is really a paradoxical statement. It aims at dramatizing the difficulty of maintaining silence. To be *creatively silent* calls for effort and self-discipline.

Much popular music today gives the impression that the musicians have united in a tremendous blast of noise endeavoring to discover how much punishment the human ear can stand. Looking rather skeptically over my son's guitar music I was surprised to encounter a song, "The Sound of Silence." One stanza of this musical masterpiece reads:

> Hello darkness, old friend, I've
> come to talk with you again,
> Because a vision softly creeping left
> its seeds while I was sleeping
> And the vision that was planted
> in my brain still remains written the
> *Sound of Silence.*[1]

Amid all the din of rock and roll comes a somewhat distorted but plaintive plea for a memory of long ago, "The Sound of Silence."

I once watched a beautiful religious movie. Photographed in color, it portrayed before us the breathtaking beauties of outstanding scenic spots of the North American continent. In the background a gifted singer rendered the song, "This is My Father's World." The lovely scenery was a pictorial commentary on the song.

It will probably horrify teachers of small children in religious schools when I express my doubts as to the validity of the movie's underlying thesis that God is easily discovered in the beauties of nature. In my visits to the parts of the country noted for their scenery I have seldom been impressed by the depth of religious devotion of the inhabitants.

On the other hand, trips to the sandy plains of West Texas have sent me home pondering the religious dedication of so many people in those areas. Great numbers of these churches, crowded to the doors on Sundays, are located in country which has a peculiar charm that grows on people but would not be considered beautiful by many. I am sometimes tempted to claim there is an inverse ratio of religious devotion to natural beauty.

The desert may offer us a clue to it all. A good proportion of the great religions of the world have arisen in the East. Judaism, Christianity, Islam either came into existence, or were nurtured, in the silent sands of the desert. Here it was that Moses saw the burning bush, Jesus overcame temptation, Mahomet had his vision, Paul thought out the implications of his new found faith.

Void of distraction, the desert provided the silent environment within which a man could clearly hear the voice of deity.

Some monastic orders lay upon their members the vow of silence. The assumption is that only when the monks are quiet can they really hear the voice of God.

I sometimes smile when I hear ministers saying they need a new auditorium which will be "more worshipful." The assumption is that a new type of building will make all the difference in creating a worshipful atmosphere. In my late adolescence I occasionally worshipped with the Plymouth Brethren. Meeting in the barest halls, the only adornment being inartistic signs carrying Scripture verses, they had the most worshipful services I have ever attended.

Silence was the key to it all. No organist in whispered conferences, pushing or pulling stops, beamed smiling messages. Greeting, giggling, whispering, shuffling were all outlawed. Coughing was hushed by the miracle drug, reverence. Children were quieted. People tiptoed in to take their places in the circle to sit with heads bowed or reading their Bibles. The keen anticipation of the movement of the Spirit of God in leading one of the assembled laymen to announce a hymn, read the Scripture, or offer prayer was sensed in these moments of deep reverence which contrasted with the hubbub of many Protestant services. Their secret was the use of silence.

Varieties of Silence

Lest I create the wrong impression, let me hasten to point out that all silence is not of equal value. The sound of silence brings a variety of messages and speaks with any of a number of voices.

The *silence of retreat* is the sulking attitude which says, "All right, I'll just cut myself off from you and I'll wear you down by refusing to talk." This emotional curtain can isolate people as effectively as any Berlin wall.

If, by some chance, you imagine silence is passive, just wait until you encounter *defiant silence*. It fairly shouts and communicates the idea, "Okay, I am going to listen. Trot out your evidence. Let's hear if you can really tell me something." Answering defiant silence is like trying to recapture an escaped parakeet in a darkened room. The responder hardly knows where to go or what to do, with his subject determined to sidestep and keep him in a blind stumble.

The *silence of rebuke* is used effectively by a speaker I know who regularly addresses teenagers and is bothered when a couple of them start whispering to each other. As they commence to confer he stops. A deathly silence follows. People begin to look uncomfortable. Gradually the culprits understand, put innocent smiles on their faces, and gaze intently at the speaker. He takes up his talk again, having gained their attention with the silence of rebuke.

Creative Silence

Altogether different is *creative silence*. It says: "I could fill up the time with small talk, and there may even be something I could say which interests you. But this is not my purpose. I want to provide you with a situation in which you can think about yourself, your failures and shortcomings, problems, assets, and future plans. Because of my interest in you, I am willing to sit in silence with you."

Like any other creative activity, this type of silence calls for self-control and diligent practice. For most of us ten seconds of silence seems like ten hours of time. The garrulous age in which we live has made us fearful of quietude. Life is too much a carnival of noise when we may really need a chapel of silence.

The drug addict may easily be the greatest single challenge faced by psychotherapy today. He is generally a sociopathic personality who has no well-formed value system and spends a good proportion of his time manipulating people for his own selfish purposes. Efforts to help these people have been very discouraging, but a new venture instituted by enlightened court probation officers in New York is chalking up a remarkable record.

To enter the program the addict has to present himself at the "house" called Daytop Lodge. The first treatment he gets is silence. Arriving at the Lodge, he is told to take a seat and wait. He may see many of his ex-friends from the streets who are now living in the Lodge. To his dismay he discovers no one wants to talk with him. He is compelled to sit in silence and think about the commitment of life he is about to make. For him a period of silence may be the beginning point of a whole new era of living.

I once counseled a woman who told the story of her troubles with great difficulty. As she proceeded, her speed of speaking gradually built, then slowed down as her agitation subsided. Like the calm following the storm, she lapsed into silence.

After what seemed an eternity, but was probably in actual fact only a few minutes, I said, "Is there something else you would like to tell me?"

The woman looked startled and confused. Later investigation showed she had been thinking furiously, and I had interrupted her train of thought.

When we rush in to cover over the periods of silence we may hold up the redemptive process. This troubled individual may be building up her courage to make a clean breast of it all. Or she may be trying to put things together in a way that they can be expressed. She needs this situation and some time in which to do her thinking.

A troubled man went to visit his physician with a list of anxieties and fears. The wise doctor told his patient to take a day off work and visit the beach. In his hand he placed an envelope and told the man to open it when he reached his destination.

On arrival he found a quiet spot and opened the envelope. On a small piece of paper he read the words, "Listen carefully." Recounting the experience later, he told what a rewarding day it was as he heard for the first time in years the lapping of the waves, the song of the bird, and the sighing of the wind. Then he remembered a statement from Carlyle: "Silence is the element in which great things fashion themselves." He discovered the moment of silence could be the moment of revelation.

Many professional people in the psychotherapy field have come to recognize the use of silence. Reik states the situation clearly: "In psychoanalysis . . . what is spoken is not the important thing. It appears to us more important to recognize what speech conceals and what silence reveals."[2]

Anne Morrow Lindbergh has stated the situation very beautifully in her book *Gift from the Sea*.

Here on this island I had had space. . . . Here there is time; time to be quiet; time to work without pressure; time to think; time to watch the heron . . . . Time to look at the stars or to study a shell; time to see friends, to gossip, to laugh, to talk. Time, even, *not* to talk. . . . Here on the island I find I can sit with a friend without talking, sharing the day's last sliver of pale green light on the horizon, or the whorls in a small white shell, or the dark scar left in a dazzling night sky by a shooting star. The communication becomes communion and one is nourished as one never is by words.[3]

CHAPTER 7

Consider
Your Listener's Perspective

King Solomon, said to be the wisest of all men, wrote in the Book of Ecclesiastes that there was a time for every activity of man. Among other things, he said there was a time to speak and a time to keep silent. Most of us are agreed that there is a time to speak; we feel it would be a tragedy if there were not some voice upon the air, and that, we hope, our own. But Solomon said there was also a time to keep silent. About this we are not quite sure. A poet recently expressed the misgiving that often enters the heart of the listener.

> I bend a sympathetic ear
> To other people's woes,
> However dull it is to hear
> Their real or fancied throes.
> I pay to every gloomy line
> Attention undiminished,
> Because I plan to start on mine
> The moment theirs are finished.[1]

Rather unfortunately, this is the attitude of so many of us.

To be a good listener demands a certain attitude towards people. Self-centered individuals are not good listeners. The listening process demands that we enter actively into another person's thinking and try to understand just what is going on within him. The listener is actively at work trying to find out what makes his speaker tick.

During my army service in the Australian Military Forces I was witness to a strange incident. A single rank of six men was being drilled. With them marched a drummer, beating out the time for the precision maneuvers. According to the drill movement, he was sometimes in the front and at other times at the rear of the group.

As the exercise progressed, the drummer was out in front of the squad marching away from the drill sergeant. The sergeant shouted the command, "About face," and the squad executed the movement with the precision of a well-oiled machine. But not the unfortunate drummer, who, prepossessed with his rhythmic beat, had failed to hear the command and marched steadily on down the parade ground.

The sergeant yelled to the drummer until he was red in the face, but with no effect. The drummer, unaware of his solitary situation, marched steadily onward. With a gesture of frustration the sergeant finally gave up and left the lonely drummer marching down the mile-long parade ground.

Like the drummer, many of us are hard at work expressing ourselves and are so caught up in the process of our own lives that we fail to hear the voices of those who need someone to listen to them.

Making Contact

It is not always easy to make contact in communication. Radio hams trying to contact each other must work out a number of possible complications involving time or favorable weather conditions. Despite all the trouble, they sometimes find it impossible to establish contact.

Similarly, there are many problems in making contact between individuals. There is always the possibility that we will be operating on two different wavelengths and fail really to get in touch with each other.

An Englishman visited Fort Worth, Texas and traveled by train, arriving at the railroad depot on a blistering summer afternoon. His hostess waited to welcome him, crisp in her light summer dress and still cool from her air-conditioned house and automobile.

As he emerged, face red, clothes wrinkled, and wiping the perspiration from his brow, his hostess inquired if he'd had a good trip.

"I don't know if you would call it good," he replied. "As the train came down into Texas the air conditioning went out. It became hotter and hotter until at last, when we were coming into Fort Worth, it seemed as if we were being baked in an oven."

"You can say that again," responded his friendly, self-possessed hostess.

"As the train came down into Texas the air conditioning . . ."

This Englishman was a literalist. He was not familiar with that peculiar brand of American English that some Texans use.

He had been taken in by a colloquialism. The woman was really saying, "You look as if you've had a pretty rough trip, and I want to establish communication with you and make you feel at ease." They had failed to make contact.

That Pesky Early Warning System

Communication breakdown is prevented by carefully avoiding certain warning signals. Inflammatory words may be innocently slipped into conversation or deep-rooted prejudices inadvertently touched off in moments of tension.

Harry Fontain is hanging a picture for his wife. An industrious businessman, he is the despair of his mate when it comes to household chores. In fact, he rather prides himself on his lack of domestic skills and often brags that he doesn't know which end of the hammer to hold. But today it is different.

By leaving the picture in an obvious place where he had nearly fallen over it, his helpmate had been able to offer a subtle suggestion and then appear pleasantly surprised when he walked in carrying his seldom-used tools and announced his intention to "get this picture on the wall."

The little woman works hard at keeping him motivated. "Honey, that's wonderful. Not only the best businessman in the city but a handyman as well," she murmurs.

"Oh, shucks, it's nothing,"—but Harry has a pretty good feeling. "How is that? Seems like a pretty good spot to me."

He holds the picture in a trial position and awaits the final word of approval.

"Just a bit too high, honey. Mother always said you had high ideas . . ."

Harry's interest in picture-hanging evaporates. He labors through that little chore in the most halfhearted manner. "Mother always said . . ." is like waving a red flag in front of a bull.

Like so many of us, Harry has an Emotional Early Warning System. As soon as some words cross the threshold of our hearing, the red lights flash and the alarm bells begin to clang.

The very moment some Republicans hear "Democrat," or an industrialist hears "union," or there comes to our ears a name or concept about which we feel strongly, the Emotional Early Warning System goes into action.

Even such a highly developed and intricate radar system

as that spreading across North America can misinterpret a harmless object as being a threatening invader. A man's Emotional Early Warning System may be triggered by one word and prevent him from hearing the rest of the statement.

The wife's word, "mother," may fire an explosion and keep hubby from hearing that his mother-in-law has drawn her will in his favor. A message that the representative from the Internal Revenue Department would like an interview can lead to a noncooperative response which will keep the professional man from learning there is a better way to figure his income tax.

– The good listener fights down the impulsive response. He needs time to understand the other person and see the full implication of what is being said.

When you attend a social function to whom do you talk? In all probability it is to someone with interests similar to yours. Try to find someone with an altogether different background. Discover the unusual in his experiences. It will be rewarding for you, it may help him, and there is a distinct possibility you will make a new friend.

If you really aspire to listen, forget yourself! Abandon your preoccupation with your own life and affairs and seek to recognize the factors which have made this person's life what it is.

This psychological factor of overcoming our own natural self-centeredness may constitute the most difficult aspect of the whole experience. Listening may be the optimum response to the Master's command, "Let a man deny himself."

The supreme act of commitment to one's fellows can be envisaged in many ways—giving away possessions, leaving home and loved ones, undertaking arduous enterprises —or it may be seen in a willingness to listen.

CHAPTER 8

Beware of
Three Traps of Listening

I once attended a seminar conducted by an eminent sociologist. He was an authority and obviously knew his subject as did few others in his field. At the conclusion of his presentation he announced that he had come to hear as well as to speak. He invited the group members to express their opinions and ask questions about the subject under discussion.

This scientist's reactions to the people who spoke were a fascinating study in themselves. He turned his black eyes upon the somewhat verbose questioner with a beady stare as if to lull him into a hypnotic trance and, hopefully, silence. If a participant persisted, the sociologist's bushy eyebrows began a rhythmic movement like two gyrating caterpillars poking faces at one another. His rather large red lips shaped out unspoken words, occasionally reinforced by strange incoherent sounds. Ham-like hands reached out in mesmeric movements.

When he spoke it was, "Go on," but every response of his body shouted, "Keep quiet and let me talk."

If you are going to listen, you must pay attention. You should convey the impression that you are with the speaker every inch of the way. A word of caution, however, may be in order. An over-enthusiastic responder can easily open his mouth only to put his foot in it.

Three traps for the unwary listener are keeping the record straight, outguessing the speaker, and conducting a cross examination. Tragically enough, these are not the failures of the indifferent but of the over-enthusiastic, who, unwittingly, cut off their listener's ears.

Keeping the Record Straight

Any conversation is carried on in a context, and it is often necessary to have some information about the events leading up to the experiences under discussion. Some background material gives meaning to what is being related. Nevertheless, there are people whose passion for correctness and detail will bog down any effort at conversation.

Listen to Sonya and Bryant Gilmore talking with a group of their friends. Bryant is telling of an unusual experience which befell the Gilmore family on their last vacation.

Sonya's eyes are gleaming, as she too in her imagination, recalls that remarkable adventure.

"We left about the middle of July," begins Bryant.

"Not really the middle, honey," says his sweet little wife. "It was actually the 27th. . . ."

"Was it really? You know, I thought it was about the 15th or 16th; in fact, I well remember that was the day Harry Jones borrowed the lawnmower. . ."

The story is half ruined already. The listener begins to wonder inwardly if the Gilmores will ever get away on their trip.

Having failed to settle the date, Mr. Gilmore, just a little red in the face, plunges into his story, with Mrs. Gilmore hovering around like a vulture looking for fresh opportunities for prey.

"We threw in our lines and in no time flat the fish were almost jumping into the boat. Within twenty minutes we had a big mess of fish. There must have been fifty fish on the string by the time we stopped."

"Oh, honey, you know there were only thirty-five."

"Thirty-five! Why I caught twenty-five myself, and Johnnie and Jimmy must have easily landed another twenty-five between them."

Mrs. Gilmore heaves a sigh and looks apologetically at the company. "That's my husband! Always multiplies the number by two to make it sound good."

So the conversation goes on with Mr. Gilmore's annoyance index rapidly rising. He finally glares at his wife and lapses into silence.

Mrs. G., having made sure that every minute detail is correct and now vaguely aware of her spouse's antagonism, finally decides to retire to the kitchen to prepare a snack.

What did it matter whether they left for their vacation on July 11, 16, or 27, or whether they caught 29 or 50 fish? These were side issues of no importance to the auditors.

By insisting on the minutiae, Mrs. Gilmore had annoyed and frustrated her husband, embarrassed the visitors, and generally cast a shadow on the evening.

The Outguesser

I have a friend who is a real intellect. Bright, quick, and sharp, I always used to delight in meeting her. But something strange happens when we begin to talk.

As the conversation proceeds I get the funny feeling that I don't know my own mind. My friend works too hard. She won't ever let me complete a statement. Committed to helping me, she is so enthusiastic that I sometimes feel like pleading, "Please don't help me so much."

I begin to tell her about the airplane trip I had to New York. "I was running late as I set out to the airport and when I arrived . . ."

"You had to wait at the ticket counter."

"No, the ticket counter was OK, but . . ."

It's the same with almost any subject we discuss. I start; she guesses what I am going to talk about and tries to help. The main problem is that her guesses are generally *wrong*.

How I dread that familiar gleam she gets in her eye. That signal tells me she is about to take over.

I pondered the problem for a long time. It is hard to tell someone about an unfortunate habit that characterizes her life. Some people are so easily hurt that it ruins a friendship. Should I continue to put up with Jean? Or should I speak?

Then I realized my good-natured intervention might completely alter the course of her life. I could see her in a future day taking me to one side to murmur gratefully, "Thank you so much, John. If you hadn't been brave enough to tell me I might have still been interrupting people."

I took her out to lunch—to Neiman-Marcus. We ate *her* favorite—frog legs; I cannot bear them myself. They might *taste* like chicken but I know they are not.

She relaxed in her chair. "Well, John, what was it you wanted to talk to me about?"

I swallowed hard, plucked up my courage, and launched into the supreme effort to change the whole style of Jean's personality.

"Jean, how do you feel about people who interrupt . . .?"

"I think it is an awful thing for one person to interrupt another when he is speaking. Of course, it is different if you go to his rescue. If you really know some poor person is trying to say something and can't get it out you have a moral obligation to help them. . . ."

So I am reduced to avoiding Jean. When I see her coming I sometimes wistfully think it would be nice to talk with her, but I just cannot bear to think of starting out on so many conversational journeys that will never be completed.

Don't outguess. You might be wrong.

The Cross-Examiner

The cross-examiner is like the famous Sergeant Friday of television fame whose oft-repeated statement was, "I only want the facts." These human fact-finders can slow down any conversation.

One year it was my privilege to visit Pelican Island on the Indian River. It was a tremendous experience.

We boarded an air boat, skimmed along inches above the water and saw the island covered with pelicans rising in a noisy, flapping cloud at our approach. Guided by the game warden, we peeped at nests and had eyeball contact with babies as big as eagles. We marvelled at the ecological wonder of the cycle of fish providing food for pelicans, who, in turn, fertilized the surrounding waters, causing the multiplication of marine life.

Ruth should be told about this. She is a member of the Audubon Society, an avid birder. As I thought of her I mentally resolved she would be the first person I'd contact when I arrived home.

Scarcely recovered from the trip, I picked up the phone to dial Ruth's number.

"Ruth, this is John."

"Oh, hello, John."

"Ruth, I had a wonderful experience. While I was in Florida I took a trip in an air boat to Pelican Island and saw the one place where pelicans nest in great numbers."

"Were they white pelicans or brown pelicans?"

"I don't know."

"You don't know! Didn't your guide explain to you about the different types and colors?"

"Well, no, they all looked sort of dirty."

"The white pelican has a wing of about nine feet, the brown only about six feet. The white pelican flies with its head kind of hunched back. If it plunges into the water when seeking its food, it would be a brown pelican. On the other hand, if it were a white pelican, it would scoop up fish while it was swimming. Does that help you, John?"

"Er . . . yes. Oh, Ruth, there is someone at the door. Why don't I call you back later?"

Ruth's cross-examining had thoroughly demoralized me.

There is all the difference in the world between a district attorney's fighting for justice, struggling to get the truth out of a reticent criminal, and a person's trying to encourage a conversation with another. Your subject is not likely to be an enthusiastic talker if he feels he is on trial for perjury or being given an oral examination for a Ph.D. degree.

Fight back every urge you have to learn the details, outguess the speaker, or cross-examine your subject. Make your choice. You can be an expert on details, a gifted outguesser, or a skillful cross-examiner. In fact, you can be any combination of these, but you cannot at the same time be a good listener.

CHAPTER 9

Cultivate
The Skill of Reply

We have already noted the importance of not interrupting or breaking up the flow of the speaker's conversation. There is danger in taking this counsel too literally. If the listener just sits and stares or has a blank, expressionless face, he may accomplish nothing. There needs to be an indication that the speaker is not addressing his remarks to a propped-up cadaver and that there is some evidence of a breath of life within the listener's passive body.

The effective listener must learn the skill of a reply which indicates he is intensely interested in all that is being said. A second and equally important function of the reply is as a pump primer aimed at stimulating and facilitating the flow of speech and the expression of feelings and ideas.

The Short Reply

The taciturn Jim was sitting with his loquacious girl friend, Nancy. It was a summer evening with romance in the air. The conversation took a more intimate turn.

NANCY: Do you think I have dainty little fingers?

JIM: Sure.

NANCY: Do you feel my voice is like the song of the nightingale?

JIM: Sure.

NANCY: When you look into my eyes do they seem like
            deep blue springs?

JIM: Sure.

NANCY: Oh, Jim. What lovely things you think to say.

Jim was the master of the short reply. He had gradually
discovered that most people want to be encouraged to speak.

A peep into a counseling situation may show how the
short reply is used by some counselors.

Mr. Tyler: . . . and I don't need anybody telling me what
            is wrong with me. I feel rotten enough these
            days.

Counselor: Rotten?

By his short reply and the inflection of his voice the counselor has issued an invitation for Mr. Tyler to continue.

Discussing what they call "nondirective listening," Nichols and Stevens make an eloquent plea for the short reply.
They maintain the best responses in listening are short and
pithy and contain within them a request to keep talking.

These authorities dogmatically advise aspiring listeners,
"Employ three kinds of verbal reactions only." One of these
is utilizing the words "Hmmm," "Uh-huh," "Oh," or "I see."[1]

The best responses are sometimes described as a series of
"eloquent and encouraging grunts." Note particularly the
words "eloquent" and "encouraging." It is the grunt accom-
panying earnest solicitation for more information.

Reflection Replies

My first encounter with a tape recorder was traumatic, and
the moment remains as an indelible imprint on my mind. So
much trouble had gone into the preparation and delivery of
that sermon. I sat with my wife for my moment of triumph.

We were filled with wonder at this miracle of electronics

as it started to speak to us. But it was no triumph. The words were familiar; but the sound! This wretched machine was distorting my golden voice.

Turning to my wife I asked, "Isn't there something wrong with that tape recorder? I don't really sound like that, do I, honey?"

To my horror my cute little wife replied, "Darling, it's just exactly like you."

Because of the way the voice is produced, it obviously sounds differently to me from the way my audience hears it. I don't really know how I sound. And this doesn't only apply to sound. It may apply to content as well as the emotional overtones of what is being said.

A reflective response helps the speaker understand what he is really saying. These replies can be conveniently classified as interrogative, clarifying, repetitive, and "information please" responses.

The Interrogative Reply

This type of response says in effect, "I am very interested in what you are saying, but I think you mean something not obvious in your statement."

Mike Simmons is discussing his work and complaining bitterly about some of his fellow employees. Then he moves over to speaking about his expense account.

Mike: They've got plenty of money. When you look at the president's salary and some of those vice presidents', I don't mind padding my expense account. Just put an extra ten dollars here and there. Some times I make as much as fifty dollars on a trip.

Counselor: Do you feel all right about doing this?

Mike: Oh, heck, it's nothing. Everybody does it . . . It's stupid, but I do get a bit worried about it as to whether it is the right thing to do.

Counselor: You sometimes have a second thought about its rightness or wrongness?

Mike is obviously having a struggle with himself and covering up by saying it doesn't matter because everybody does it. He may need to explore the whole area of his values a little further.

The Clarifying Reply

A response in this category implies, "I think I get the message you are trying to pass on to me. You mean thus and so. Is this right?"

Harry Simmons has come to visit his minister. In middle adolescence, he is having difficulties in resolving his relationship with his mother.

Harry: I know my mother has made a lot of sacrifices for me so that I can go to college, but I get so mad about some of the silly things she does.
Pastor: Silly things?
Harry: She sits me down and tries to get me to tell her everything about school—all the silly little things that don't really matter. She keeps on until I get mad at her. I tell her I'm not going to come home again. I know it's foolish because I really owe so much to her. But she has no right to treat me as though I were still a little kid.
Pastor: You really love and appreciate her, but there are times when you almost feel as if you hate her.

Harry has what some psychologists call "ambivalent feelings." This is an uncomfortable state of mind in which we feel two ways about something. The good listener can render a service by helping to clarify these two-way feelings.

The Repetitive Reply

The connotation of this response is, "It's nice of you to

tell me this. I'm not going to block you. I really want to hear what you have to say. Tell me more."

Although often the subject of good-natured banter, one of the most effective techniques of response is to reflect the last statement of the speaker.

> *Mrs. Jones:* You know, pastor, I've been coming to this church for a long time, but of recent days I've been disappointed. When I look back on those earlier days, I can see it used to be different.
> *Pastor:* Used to be different?

In this simple phrase is the invitation to continue even though what is being stated may be critical.

The "You're Not Making It Clear" Reply

The listener is telling the speaker, "It's hard to keep up with you. You're familiar with the subject but I'm not sure I understand all you mean. Let's try again."

Mr. Jones is listening to Sid Harris tell his story. The story gets more and more involved until at last Jones feels he must say something.

> *Harris:* Then this older brother of mine persuaded our second cousin to put all the money in the mortgage of the house, and that led to all this other trouble.
> *Jones:* Just a moment. Let's get all this sorted out. How do these people relate to your problem with your wife?"

While there is a danger that too much attention to detail will derail the conversation, an occasional question tells the speaker he is being followed in his narrative.

In Defoe's immortal story of Robinson Crusoe, he depicts the awful loneliness of a man living on a solitary island. When the isolation became unbearable, Crusoe would make his way to a certain valley into which he could shout and then hear his voice come echoing back to him.

Like Crusoe, many of us really want to know what we are saying. The listener skilled in the art of reply becomes a sounding board, an echo chamber, and through the experience of being listened to, the troubled person often discovers himself anew.

CHAPTER 10

Ask a Question—
But Do It Carefully

A group of men sat in a barber's shop, gazing into space, each thinking his own thoughts and inwardly hoping his turn for tonsorial attention might soon arrive.

The bright-eyed youth smiled as he entered, took his seat, and surveyed the zombies lining the wall.

After a few futile efforts to get a conversation started, he addressed a question to the farthest barber, "How would you like to work on just heads without bodies?"

The barber pondered a moment and chuckled. Some of the waiting customers looked up. At the end of the shop, a man, obviously anxious to get back to his work, interjected a thought, "Maybe they'll come up with an idea that will let people leave their heads at the shop while they continue their job at the office."

The sandy-haired youth in the center joined in, "Wouldn't it be good if you could get a spare head?"

A man whose small edging of fluff around the periphery of baldness only barely justified his presence in the shop wistfully commented, "It might even be possible to trade in your head on a new one."

In short order a stimulating conversation was under way. Strangers were talking to each other, smiling and laughing.

On one side sat the youth who had started it all. He said nothing, just smiled with a quiet satisfaction. He was now the listener who had started a fascinating conversation with one "way-out" inquiry.

An imaginative question had universal appeal. The harassed barbers, trying to keep up their work, and the long-suffering customers, thinking of all they needed to do, were all ready to respond to an unusual question.

The late President Kennedy was widely known for his witty answers to questions fired at him. It is not such common knowledge that he also had a peculiar ability to ask an incisive question and pay unusual attention to what was said to him. Robert Saudek conferred with the President while producing the television series, "Profiles in Courage," and later reported: "He made you think he had nothing else to do except ask you questions and listen—with extraordinary concentration—to your answers. You knew that for the time being he had blotted out both the past and the future. More than anyone else I have ever met, President Kennedy seemed to understand the importance of *now*."[1]

"The importance of now" is a phrase which conveys the skill of the questioner. His subject becomes vividly aware of this moment when he has something special to contribute in response to the question.

Posing The Query

While the question is undoubtedly the simplest technique for getting a conversation under way, there is no guarantee that a rote question will necessarily change a sour puss into a compulsive talker. Each type of question has a possibility, but beware of the pitfalls.

Suppose you are left in the room with your mother's aunt's second cousin. He is an unlikely prospect as a candidate for a talk fest, but mother is so anxious he be made to "feel at home." Before leaving the room she had batted her eyelids at you in a way that said, "Please do your best."

A situation like this calls for all you've got. You can start off with the good old *Hometown Pride Standby,* "Where do you come from?"

He may answer, "Well, I came from Chicago yesterday."

Resist all the urges to point out the crass stupidity of this answer and elucidate, "I really meant the town you call home."

This type of question seeks to arouse the "breathes there a man with soul so dead" spirit, and it usually can spark a conversation. It is possible he will proceed to point out that he doesn't really call any place home; he has wandered around so many different parts of the country. Recounting this odyssey will fill in a fair amount of time, and relieve the previous strain.

Maybe the effort will fail. He doesn't want to talk about the town where he grew up, and he gives you the stop light, "There was an unfortunate incident . . ."

Now is the time to try the *Alma Mater Technique.* You say, "What school did you attend?"

Don't make the mistake of using the word graduate. He may have had only a summer there, but when you leave the question in its innocuous form he can conveniently murmur Yale, Harvard, or Princeton, and you can respond with a statement about how marvellous it must have been to *work* at an Ivy League School.

That word *work* will let him out. He may never have had a course there, but if he served as a plumber or a janitor it does the trick.

Then there is the appellation, "school." It has a merciful elasticity. If he never attended college he can murmur the

name of a high or an elementary school. If he finally gets to
kindergarten it might be well to try another line of questioning.

The Vocational Inquiry has possibilities. It is asked with
the knowledge that there are over six thousand different jobs
listed in the U. S. Handbook of Occupations and based on
the assumption that most people work.

So you say, "Where do you work?"

If he looks the professional type you may pose it as, "Who
are you with?"

If he has the appearance of being neither altogether pro-
letarian or bourgeois, it may be more appropriately stated
as, "How do you earn your daily bread?"

Most people spend so much of their time at work that they
are generally happy to hold forth about their occupation, its
frustrations and rewards, for a considerable length of time.
On the other hand, he may screw up his face with a "please
don't talk about that" look and you are driven back to another approach.

The Kith and Kin Investigation may be useful. You start
off by saying, "Are you married?"

Supposing he responds, "yes," all types of avenues open
up as you discuss wife and children. You may even stumble
upon a grandfather. Just remember there are dolts, idiots,
and grandparents. Forget about conversation, and brace
yourself for stories and pictures, especially pictures.

If you don't do any good with the family approach you
may have to use the *Help Method*. Your sex may be a disad-
vantage. Men are not particularly good in using the help
method.

My wife has a strange female quirk. When we are travelling she imagines the best way to find the correct route is
to "ask somebody." I know, of course, that a map is all I need.

As I am struggling with my map-reading, she coyly suggests, "Why don't you ask somebody?"

I respond, "Honey, I have a perfectly good map prepared by the American Automobile Association. They ought to know. I really don't need any help."

And this is the way it goes on until I finally give in and ask, only to discover I am miles out of my way and would have saved an hour if I had only asked earlier.

Although I have a built-in resistance to this method of automobile navigation and I feel we should not bother any other person, our inquiries have always been graciously received, for there is nothing more appealing than someone who is seeking help.

"I need help. I have absolutely no knowledge about astronomy, and yet I'd love to know something about satellites. . . ." With words similar to these beamed at the subject's special knowledge, many a clammed-up individual has been persuaded to unbend.

Offer To Help

An offer to be of assistance may also have a subtle magic. But let it be done sincerely. The tongue-in-cheek attitude is too often represented by the office inscription, "May I help you out? Which way did you come in?"

To sincerely reach out a helping hand to a troubled person may easily open up a channel of communication.

I often talked at length with my grandfather. Nothing remarkable about that, you might think, but you obviously didn't know my granddaddy. A medium-sized, wrinkled, suntanned individual with a straight back, he wore a luxuriant crop of fascinating mutton-chop whiskers. He was, to put it mildly, a man of few words. Compared with him Calvin Coolidge must have been a compulsive talker.

Addressed by most of the family as "Dah," a name whose origin was long ago lost, he was a hard worker who believed actions spoke louder than words. He seldom talked with his twelve children, evidently believing the provision of bread and lodging told the story.

His meals were eaten in stony silence. Immediately following the completion of supper he saddled and mounted his horse, riding at a leisurely pace to the small country store where he sat in the corner and listened to the other farmers talk.

The only consistent sound I ever heard from him came after he had retired to his room. The victim of an asthmatic condition, he used some sort of atomizer device which puffed up pressure, hissing the misty medicine into his lungs.

The sound from my hitherto silent relative mystified and fascinated me. I sometimes wondered if he were pumping himself up before sallying forth to work in the fields or visit the country store.

In my eleventh year, as always, we made our annual visit to my grandfather's farm. After a year in the city I was anxious to get down to the open fields where Granddaddy was harvesting the alfalfa.

The smell was *so* good. My grandfather had cut the crop, and now he raked it away, piling it into heaps ready for pitching up onto the cart.

With boyish enthusiasm I greeted him, to be answered by a noncommittal grunt. Taking a breather on a shady side of the cart, he looked hot and tired. As he poured some water from a canvas water bag into the tin cup, I felt sorry for him, so I asked, "Can I help you, Grandpa?"

He looked a little stunned at first but kind of half nodded his permission. Anxious to work off the boredom of that long train ride, I gave all my boyish energy to raking up that lovely, sweet-smelling alfalfa. Later on I climbed up on the cart while he pitched it up to me and I pushed it into the corners, jumping around and having the time of my life.

From that day on we were the best of friends. One evening as we sat on the front porch of the farm house he was reading the advertisements in the paper. Peering through his magnifying glass, he addressed a rare question to me, "I wonder what them kippered snakes taste like?"

Puzzled at the thought of some enterprising company's putting snakes in cans, I walked over and looked at the paper. My youthful eyes rapidly read and I leaned over and whispered, "Grandpa, that's kippered snacks."

A rare smile came over his face and he patted my hand in a gesture of appreciation. After that he often asked me to check up on things not too clear to his aging eyes.

I felt very proud of my new found position. I often rode with him on the farm cart. The other members of the family wondered at this strange relationship and why he should have chosen me to talk to.

One day my uncle, who was himself quite a talker, challenged Grandpa as to why he talked to John. Grandpa puffed on his pipe for a while before answering, "Maybe because he asked me if he could help me."

Beware of Yes or No

The best conversation openers don't just seek out facts. They focus on the feelings of the subject and seek to help him get down to his emotional reactions, opinions, ideas.

One simple rule of thumb for opening conversation with questions is never to ask a question which can be answered by "yes" or "no" unless you have a follow-up query ready.

You are talking with Jim Jones, who seems to be greatly troubled by family relationships.

One way of approaching it would be to say, "Do you like living with your brother?"

This will probably invite an answer of "yes" or "no," and you will sit there looking at each other.

Another better way would be to say, "How do you feel about living with your brother?" This may evoke his feelings and ideas and stimulate his response.

Interrogation of Questions

Try out your powers of questioning. In the following questions some are good and some poor. Check ($\vee$) the good ones, (X) the poor ones.

1. Did you have a good day today? ( )
2. How do you feel about this? ( )
3. Do you like your work? ( )
4. Have you any ideas on the subject? ( )
5. "Oh, really?" ( )
6. Would you explain this to me? ( )
7. Will you accept the new offer? ( )
8. What is your reaction to this situation? ( )
9. Do you love me? ( )
10. Please give me your opinion on the subject. ( )

After you have concluded turn to page 72 for the correct answer.

Writing under the heading, *"Ask, Don't Tell,"* a recent writer concluded there were guidelines for effective questioning.

- Take every possible chance to ask a searching question, *then keep quiet.* (When you're talking, you're not learning anything.)
- One thoughtful question is worth a dozen inquisitive ones. The prod-and-pry approach makes people clam up.

- Questions that come close to the other person's true interest get the best answers—provided you are interested too.
- Be prepared to wait. Sometimes a long silence can be more rewarding than another question.
- *In every case*, the quality of an answer depends on the quality of attention given by the questioner.
- Questions must spring from honest inquiry, not from attempts at flattery or efforts to manipulate the other person's thinking.
- Questions that deal with a person's *feelings* are more provocative than those that deal with *facts*.[2]

Harry Emerson Fosdick, the celebrated preacher, was asked the secret of posing a good question. His reply was,

"I suppose the secret, if there is one, is to realize that questioning and listening are inseparable. The asking of good questions represents listening on its highest plane, and that of course can never be faked or turned on—it must come from within. I believe it's the quality of attention that makes all the difference."[3]

Ask a question—but do it carefully.

*Answer to the test on page 71.

Questions 1, 3, 5, 7, 9, are poor because they can be answered with a non-commital "yes" or "no."

Questions 2, 4, 6, 8, 10, are better. They stimulate further conversation.

PART TWO

ADVENTURES IN LISTENING

CHAPTER 11

The Eclipse of Listening

~~~~~~

Whatever happened to listening?

It used to be an honorable and commendable activity, the mark of courtesy and gentility. Now this time-honored process has suffered an eclipse, and listening has almost become a dirty word.

One study carried out with sixty-eight people of varied occupational backgrounds showed that the biggest proportion of their waking moments, about seventy-five percent, was spent in the communication process. Splitting communication into the two natural divisions of speaking and listening, the investigation revealed that the average person spent about thirty percent of his time talking, and forty-five percent listening.

According to this evidence we spend more time listening than we do at anything else. The logical conclusion would be that a person who learned by experience would bend every effort of his being towards becoming adept and skillful at carrying on this primary human activity.

Investigation indicates far otherwise and shows this fundamental function of men and women is poorly carried out.

In a series of listening tests the participants attended lectures and at the conclusion were examined to find out what proportion of the lecture material they had retained. Although these were professional people, it was discovered they could recall only about fifty percent of what they had heard.

The findings were the more startling because the test was given immediately after the listening experiences. There is no telling what the results might have been if the tests were given a month, or even a week later.

If a man went to his doctor to tell him he retained only half the food that was fed to him, the physician would be alarmed and take steps to remedy the situation. Yet this same man loses more than half the information passed on to him, and nobody is concerned.

Suppose he is a college student. If he were so physically ill that he could attend only half his classes, he would probably seek permission to drop the course and ask for a refund of his fees. However, indifferent listening skills will cause him to lose more than half the material verbally presented by his teacher. In terms of economics, his impaired comprehension might conservatively be estimated to cost him a thousand dollars or more a year, and, considered as time spent in an inefficient activity, it amounts to a big segment of life which can never be recaptured.

The cost to industry of poor listening must reach astronomical figures. A sales clerk approaches a customer who asks to see a dacron shirt with *short sleeves*. The clerk begins to search frantically for a *long-sleeved* shirt but cannot find it. He consults with his supervisor who joins in the hunt with no better success. In desperation, the supervisor says he will special-order a shirt for the customer. Already overburdened, he takes time to fill out a form and airmail it to the warehouse.

Smile on his face, the clerk returns to tell the good news to the not-so-patiently waiting customer, "We have no long-sleeved dacron shirts at the moment but we are special-ordering one..."

The customer, with mounting aggravation, reminds the clerk she asked for a *short*-sleeved shirt. He hurries back to the rack and gets the short-sleeved shirt. The customer is irritated, the clerk has wasted forty-five minutes, the supervisor has spent valuable time he should have used on other important work, and the unwanted special-ordered shirt will probably clutter the store shelves. The total cost of this unnecessary operation easily eats up more than the profit of the sale.

In many retailing organizations management is realizing it is not enough for their sales personnel to be fast talkers. New employees are being trained in listening techniques. The first important rule is "listen before you act."

Even employees in such an efficient organization as the telephone company make mistakes in their listening. It is interesting to place a person-to-person long distance call, and hear the operator as she tracks down the party. I had often wondered why they let the originating party hear all that was taking place. It suddenly dawned on me that, as skilled as these operators are, accents, jumbled words, slurred numbers sometimes cause them to make mistakes. When listening, the caller is able to check up on the operator as to whether she really heard what he said, and it helps to save time for both the caller and the company.

In penetrating analysis of the existing jury system, a recent writer points out a number of defects in the procedure. One of his targets is the testimony of witnesses. According to this attorney, who has spent a lifetime in courts, most witnesses interpret any event in terms of their own background, age, race, nationality, sex, profession, religion. He quotes the example of the insecure professor who hears the phrase, "ten year plan," as the "tenure plan." His conclusion is that ". . . most people only hear what they want to hear."

The long and short of this lawyer's criticism is that in many instances we have poor witnesses because they are poor listeners. Even the course of justice may be impeded by poor listening.

Listening and Learning

It has been said, "Listening is the lost 'L' in learning." The emphasis of modern educational procedures is on expression, and, by implication, against listening. Educationalists recall with horror the days when good children were "seen and not heard," and they have ushered us into a new and wonderful era of feverish, noisy action geared to our activist society.

A silent student in a modern classroom obviously has a "personality problem." Everything is done to "draw him out" and motivate him towards the goal of "self-expression." If he speaks up and contributes, all is well. He may not really have anything to say, but he has expressed himself.

After many years of teaching, I have reached the conclusion that much "self-expression" is a mere undisciplined babble with little profit for anybody. On the other hand, some researchers have suggested that listening might be the very activity to further and expand the knowledge of a person anxious to learn.

- Certain information must be acquired. It is not a natural inherent possession. There are basic ideas and concepts to be comprehended. Some subjects like music appreciation, speaking skills, and languages, can only be learned by careful listening.

- Written materials may appear to be dull, boring, or un-interesting until we hear them verbalized. Read a Shake-spearean play and struggle to catch its spirit. Then listen to one of the fine recordings of a gifted actor speaking the part and you may find it difficult to believe it is the same material. The actor's voice breathes life into the cold print.

- A lecturer may have spent years researching a given field of knowledge. He has sifted the wheat from the chaff, gar-nered information from many sources, and consolidated it into a cohesive, logical presentation. When we learn to listen we stand to gain information it would take years of reading to gather.

- There is a time lag in disseminating knowledge. After an author has gathered his information, written it down, edited it, had it appraised and accepted by a publisher, it often takes a year for it to come out in book form. Much of the information in a newly published book is already dated. The lecturer has access to journals, studies, and re-ports, or even work in progress, and can make this fresh information available to his listeners.

- If we are listening to a good speaker, there is an interplay of speaker and listener. The cold print of a book depends on the reader alone. If he cannot understand he may just give up. The skillful speaker is constantly sensing and re-sponding to his listeners' reactions. Aware that he is above his hearers' heads, he can adapt his material to them.

- The listener can ask questions of the authority. The on-the-spot questions make immediate clarification possible.

After a reaction to, and a swing away from sterile, indoc-trinating teaching techniques which allowed no place for pupil participation, we moved into the activity phase—almost activity for its own sake. Now we must realize it cannot be physical activity alone. It must be mental participation, an involvement which can never be meaningful if there is no active listening process.

The Need For a Listening Ear

There are two aspects of the practice of listening. As we have already noted, a human must listen if he is to have contact with and know the world around him. A second, and related, need is for someone to listen to him and allow him to express himself.

William James once described his day as a "megaphonic era." What would he say of this present day in which many a harassed citizen has to resort to ear plugs in an effort to obtain an undisturbed night's rest? With all this noisemaking the troubled individual may wonder if anyone will ever hear him out.

Nestled in the heart of the city of Sydney, Australia, is a very attractive area of park land known as the Sydney Domain. Nicely located in the proximity of Port Jackson, the beautiful Sydney harbor, it has a peculiar and distinctive charm. The main attraction is to be found on a Sunday afternoon when many Sydneyites visit the Domain.

It is an enormous open forum. Everybody who has a message he feels the world must hear, a pet idea, a chip on his shoulder, makes his way to the Domain. He sets up his soap box, climbs up, and proceeds to get it "off his chest."

The Domain makes an unusual sight as little knots of people gather around the various speakers. Most visitors wander around listening for a few minutes to a speaker, then move on to the next would-be orator. Some heckle, and some interject or ask questions, frequently giving rise to good-natured and sometimes heated encounters.

There is the usual crop of crackpots, faddists, and fools in the Domain, but every man can have his say.

The number of people who take their soap boxes and stand to deliver themselves to every passing stranger may itself be mute evidence of the need for a listening ear.

The distractions and difficulties may be modern but the problem has long been with us. A poet has said:

> Listen to me for a day—an hour!—a moment!
> lest I expire in my terrible wilderness, my
> lonely silence! O God, is there no one to listen?

The poet Seneca wrote these words. He was a bright, old Roman born in 4 B.C. who, in response to the order of the Emperor Nero in A.D. 65, died by his own hand.

Apparently it was ever thus. Most people, ancient or modern, at some time or another, yearn for a listening ear.

Evidence mounts to indict our garrulous generation. Pouring out our smog of verbiage, we have beclouded a simple technique which could improve learning, make jurisprudence more efficient, and help our fellowman cope with the vicissitudes of life. Let us hope that, like the scholars of the Middle Ages who, unearthing ancient Greek manuscripts, rediscovered the magnificence of ancient knowledge, we may come to a new appreciation of an old skill.

CHAPTER 12

The Public Relations
Technique Nobody Mentions

Jean was an attractive girl. Tastefully dressed, she had soft, fair hair and the loveliest, pale-blue eyes. To her natural beauty she added the rare ingredient of intelligence. Every time the University Honors List appeared Jean's name was sure to be either at the top or nearby.

She had plenty of competition in the large university she attended. Many of the girls were more beautiful than Jean, more expensively dressed. And intelligence doesn't always help a girl with males, who like to feel their dates look up to their superior maculine wisdom.

Despite this, Jean had more men trying to date her than almost any other girl. Men gathered around her like bees at a honey pot. Deeply religious, she specialized in "church dates." She attended every service of the church and generally came escorted by an athlete or some other campus notable.

At social functions the men gravitated towards her, frequently leaving her equally attractive sisters to spend time in feminine company.

As her pastor, and a psychologist as well, I felt this psychological phenomenon was worthy of investigation. I made arrangements for Jean to come by my office for a conference.

Formalities done with, I said, "Now, Jean, tell me about yourself—where you come from, the high school you attended, your major field of study, and what you plan to be."

Jean turned those big blue eyes on me, "Why, pastor, I have lived such an ordinary existence and you have travelled the world, why don't you tell me something about yourself?"

Naturally, I wanted to help the girl, and so I launched into an account of my experiences while she hung on my every word. And the intensity of those large, light blue eyes! They were so appealing that I once forgot what I was saying.

I didn't learn much about Jean's background, field of study, or ambitions, but I discovered her secret. Her unusual attractiveness lay in her capacity to listen.

Sometime after my encounter with Jean I was reading an article in a magazine in which the writer told of some memorable advice from her mother. The daughter, preparing for her first big social event, was taken aside by her mother, who had grown up in the southern-belle tradition. The mother offered some wise counsel. "Try to get your beau to do the talking, my dear. Most men can't resist a girl who asks leading questions and pays rapt attention to their answers."

"The feminine asking role goes all the way back," she said. "It probably accounts for the Queen of Sheba's dazzling conquest of King Solomon. You remember in the Second Book of Chronicles it says she 'communed with him of all that was in her heart. And Solomon told her all her questions.' "[1]

It was a simple suggestion but very appropriate for the apprehensive debutante. If this were in any way typical of the guidance Southern mothers gave their daughters, it might be more than half the reason for the traditional charm of the southern girl.

John Wesley, the founder of Methodism, was very attractive to women who delighted in his presence but few of them ever struck a responsive chord within him. One who did was Sophy Hopkey.

Wesley met Sophy in Georgia and was immediately attracted to her. A year after the pathetic conclusion of it all he took his pen in hand and wrote a frank account of their relationship. As he penned this remarkable story he revealed at least one reason why Sophy cast such a spell over him.

In his description of the sweet, young girl he says, "Another thing I was much pleased in her was, that whenever we were conversing or reading, there was such a stillness in her in the whole behavior, scarce stirring hand or foot, that she seemed to be, all but her attention, dead."[2]

A good proportion of the attractiveness of Sophy for the serious-minded young minister lay in her listening ear.

When a disturbed and troubled person plucks up enough courage to visit a psychotherapist, he frequently approaches the encounter with fear and apprehension. Seated for the first time in the office, he makes a mental evaluation, while outwardly smiling to hide his inner turmoil. Inwardly he wonders, "Why ever on earth did I come here?" He speculates whether or not this is just a futile venture.

If any type of counseling is to take place, it is vital that rapport be established. Rapport is the clinician's word which means, "a comfortable and unconstrained relationship which comes to exist between two people."[3]

There are many factors which go into establishing rapport. Easily the most important of these is listening. As the counselor listens, the counselee's confidence is built, and he is able to get involved in the counseling situation.

Few men have been more successful in the field of human relations than Dale Carnegie. His book, *How to Win Friends and Influence People*, was a best seller and is still read. Carnegie's theories have been so effective that even after his death the organization he founded continues to flourish and propagate his ideas. Busy executives take time out and businessmen pay considerable sums of money to take his courses.

In one chapter of his book Carnegie discusses "An Easy Way to Become a Good Conversationalist." He tells of going to a party where a celebrated botanist was guest of honor. Carnegie asked questions about the famous man's field of study. This launched the scientist into a conversation that lasted throughout the evening.

When it was time to go, the botanist told his host that Carnegie was "a most interesting conversationalist," although Carnegie had hardly spoken a word. He tells his secret: "I had listened intently. I had listened because I was genuinely interested." Carnegie concluded: "Be a good listener. Encourage others to talk about themselves."[4]

Discussion of Carnegie's techniques generally centers on the *speaking* skills they develop. From this incident it becomes obvious he is also concerned about listening skills.

In a recent television interview Bob Hope was reminiscing and told about a cab driver he met while on a visit to New York. He climbed into the cab and gave the driver his instructions. As soon as the cabby realized the passenger was the famous entertainer he burst into song. He continued until they reached their destination. Then he cast an inquiring glance in Hope's direction.

Hope replied, "You've got a good voice. Why don't you get yourself an agent?"

The actor handed over a five-dollar bill to pay the fare on the meter, but the cabby waved him off, "Forget it. You listened."

Will that cab driver tell his children and grandchildren, "I met Bob Hope"?

I rather fancy the story will be, "Bob Hope listened to me."

There is almost a conspiracy of silence about the place of listening in public relations. But the French man La Roche-foucauld said, "We usually forgive those who bore us, but we never forgive those whom we bore." He who would establish good relationships with people must learn to listen to them.

CHAPTER 13

A Forgotten Factor in Leadership

~~~~~~

Leadership is an elusive experience among humans. There are certain unpredictable aspects about it all. Under some conditions "A" will become the leader of a group, but under different circumstances "B" will be the man. With one group "B" may be the best person, "A" with another. The particular group and the state of affairs existing at the time apparently play a large part in determining the leader.

However, there are many individuals who will never become leaders no matter what the situation. They just don't have what it takes.

Certain qualities of personality are essential in the competent leader. A fairly typical list includes physical and nervous energy, a sense of purpose and direction, friendliness and affection, integrity, technical mastery, decisiveness, intelligence, teaching skill, faith.

There is one facility absent in most of these listings of desirable leadership traits. It is listening.

The leader is almost invariably portrayed as projecting himself into his audience. His followers are anxiously waiting his word and responding to his every utterance. This is only one side of the picture. One author speaks about the necessity of the leader's making an "effective show of devotion." Such a display may take the form of a statement by the leader, but by far the most effective way to do it will be to show a willingness to listen to what his followers have to say.

The Bolshevik take-over in Russia reached a crisis point when the revolutionary dictator, Lenin, was hospitalized with a stroke, and it became evident a new leader would have to be chosen. There were two logical contenders for the position. In their concept of the leadership function they represented two entirely different approaches to the task. One was a talker, the other a listener.

The talker was Leon Trotsky, a flamboyant orator and brilliant organizer. In the early days of the revolution he had organized the Red Guard and rapidly built it into an effective fighting unit. When Lenin moved to take over the country by force of arms, he called upon Trotsky's Red Guard to secure the strongholds of the government. So successful was the armed move that the only embryonic republican form of government that Russia had ever known was effectively destroyed and a Communist dictatorship came into existence.

Pictures preserved of Trotsky show him clad in his greatcoat, standing before large gatherings of people and inspiring them with his fervent speeches. He was probably the most glamorous of all the Bolsheviks. Even his name had been taken from the jailer in Siberia from whose custody he had made his escape.

Stalin was in many ways the antithesis of Trotsky. Small in stature, with pockmarked face, by his ruthless acts of terrorism he had truly earned his name, which literally meant "Man of Steel." His cunning and craftiness had enabled him to work his way into positions of power and influence in the Bolshevik bureaucracy.

Stalin's biographer says the most striking thing about

Stalin was that there was nothing striking about him. Handicapped by his Georgian accent, he was never a very effective public speaker and realized he had to concentrate in other areas. While Trotsky was out haranguing the huge gatherings of people Stalin sat and listened. His tongue was still but his mind worked furiously.

The characteristic picture of Stalin is of his listening to every man of influence who wanted a listening ear. His biographer says, ". . . He was unsurpassed in the art of patient listening. Sometimes he would be seen in a corner of a staircase pulling at his pipe and listening immovably, for an hour or two, to an agitated interlocutor and breaking silence only to ask a few questions."[1] Sitting there, he offered a ready ear to all the Party bureaucrats who needed to get something off their chests.

Lenin's death brought to a head the struggle between Trotsky, the orator, and Stalin, the listener. The dead dictator was the idol of the revolutionaries. His body was preserved and is kept on display in Moscow to this very day. His opinion of the successor to his position would be of great importance. He had left a testament containing a damning indictment of Stalin which said in part, ". . . I propose to the comrades to find a way to remove Stalin."[2] Lenin's wife shared her husband's antipathy to Stalin, and she exercised a considerable influence among the upper echelon of the party. It seemed Stalin had been given the kiss of death.

By way of contrast, Lenin had the highest regard for the organizer of the Red Guard. His evaluation was, "Comrade Trotsky is to be sure, the most able man in the present central committee."[3] Such commendation might well have been expected to propel Trotsky into the highest office of the party.

History tells us another story. Stalin, by skillful manipulation, had Trotsky sidetracked, exiled, and finally killed by the assassin's axe. Deutscher says of Stalin, "He possessed in a high degree the gift for silence, and in this respect he was unique in a country where everybody talked far too much,"[4] and his listening technique paid off. He had established friendships and relationships with multitudes of party hacks and thus paved the way for the final intrigues opening the pathway to leadership.

The technique of listening is even more important in a democracy than in a dictatorship. Norman Rockwell, the noted artist, recounted his experiences while painting a portrait of President Eisenhower.

"The general and I didn't discuss politics or the campaign. Mostly we talked about painting and fishing. But what I remember most about the hour and a half I spent with him was the way he gave me all his attention. He was listening to *me* and talking to *me*, just as if he hadn't a care in the world, hadn't been through the trials of a political convention, wasn't on the brink of a presidential campaign."[5]

It was small wonder the General was such an effective wartime and civilian leader.

Calvin Coolidge followed a political career that ultimately led to the White House, but he was always a man of few words. On one occasion he found himself at a party seated alongside a somewhat voluble woman. She related to him that she had bet a friend she would get at least three words of conversation out of the President. Still casually looking the other way, he quietly responded, "You lose."[6]

Assessing the peculiar political skills of this taciturn man, his biographer says, he ". . . was North Hampton's champion listener; listened his way into all the offices the town would give him."[7] He continued to listen until he became Vice-President and then Chief Executive of the United States.

In his book *The Art of Listening*, published in 1958, Dominick Barbara used an illustration by making reference to a sign on the wall of a senator's office in Washington, D. C. It read, *"You ain't Learning Nothin' While You're Talkin'."*[8]

The then comparatively obscure senator was Lyndon B. Johnson of Texas—now the President of the United States.

Although he once taught speech in Texas schools, even his most enthusiastic admirers would not venture to call President Johnson a great orator. His strength apparently lies in his personal face-to-face encounters with members of Congress. One of his subordinates describes the way in which the President functions. "Does he listen? He listens so hard it's deafening."[9] Learning to listen, he acquired potent leadership skills.

While viewing a presidential press conference on television I was struck by the familiarity of the Chief Executive with the public opinion polls. In answer to a reporter's question the President was able to quote all the latest figures from the various pollsters about his foreign policy, personal popularity, and other facets of his administration. Here again was evidence of a listening ear across the nation.

In George Orwell's book *1984*, the author depicts the Communist regime in which all men are equal but some are "more equal than others." The dictator is Big Brother and in every home there is an all-seeing eye. Constant warning that "Big Brother is watching" is whispered from one to the other. In a democracy the relationship of the leader and people would better be symbolized by an *ear* in every home. It is not so much what the leader thinks of people as what the people think of the leader.

The leader who is forever talking and not taking time to listen may one day discover he has no supporters. Because he failed to listen to his followers they gave up listening to him.

Questionnaire for Executives

Nichols and Stevens have suggested a questionnaire for evaluating the listening skills of executives. Check "yes" or "no" for each of the statements.

                                                                                 Yes   No

1. As people talk to you, do you find it difficult to keep your mind on the subject at hand, to keep from taking mental excursions away from the line of thought that is being conveyed?

2. Do you listen primarily for facts, rather than ideas, when someone is speaking?

3. Do certain words, phrases or ideas so prejudice you against a speaker that you cannot listen objectively to what is being said?

4. When you are puzzled or annoyed by what someone says, do you try to get the question straightened out immediately, either in your own mind or by interrupting the talker?

5. If you feel it would take too much time and effort to understand something, do you go out of your way to avoid hearing about it?

6. Do you deliberately turn your thoughts to other subjects when you believe a speaker will have nothing particularly interesting to say?

7. Can you tell by a person's appearance

an delivery that he won't have anything   Yes   No
worthwhile to say?

8. When somebody is talking to you, do
you try to make him think you are
paying attention when you are not?

9. When you are listening to someone,
are you easily distracted by outside
sights and sounds?

10. If you really want to remember
what someone is saying, do you
try to write down most of his discourse?[10]

These authorities claim that if your answer to all these
questions is "no" you can rate yourself a good listener.

CHAPTER 14

New Medicine
For Sick Marriages

An old story, oft repeated, lists these verbal stances of a young couple: before they were married he talked and she listened; on the honeymoon, she talked and he listened; after they settled into their home they both talked and the neighbors listened. There was plenty of listening but hardly of the type likely to strengthen a marriage.

Authorities in the field of marriage counseling are agreed that communication is probably the most important single factor in maintaining a good marriage relationship. All too frequently, however, communication is thought of as talking, and there is a failure to comprehend the importance of listening in the communication process.

One wife, concerned about the problem of husband-wife relationships, told of a guessing game she played before she was married. When on a dinner date she would try to decide whether or not the other couples were husband and wife. She finally concluded that the married couples either ate in silence or with the woman talking furiously to the husband, who seemed to be enduring it in the hope that it would soon end. For this investigator lack of communication appeared to be the hallmark of marriage.

What happens to people in marriage? In dating days they

longed to talk to each other—any excuse to get together —long hours on the telephone—a subtle sort of extra sensory telegraphy system by a touch of the fingers—certain words which have a special meaning for just these two—a quick perception of a partner's statements. Then marriage comes, and, in many instances, communication slowly withers away.

There are many explanations for this change—no longer the pursuit, a more direct sexual expression, settling down to the routines of life. More important than all these is one stark reality—they have lost the motivation, inclination, or ability to listen.

One student of the subject has spoken about the "beam and murmur mechanism."[1] The writer, herself a woman, claims there is a subtle feminine secret. Apparently it is passed on from mother to daughter and so to succeeding generations.

The "beam and murmur mechanism" is used by a woman as she sits to listen to her husband. She beams at him, making strange murmuring noises of encouragement all the while. Inwardly, however, she is recalling the lovely hat she saw in the store, what she will serve at next week's party, or how she will redecorate the bedroom. After receiving some inappropriate responses, it gradually dawns on the husband that she is not really listening, and so he gives up and lapses into silence.

The same writer claims that conversation between two women is a mad race to see how much each can say before her opponent snatches the ball. Consequently, women have few scruples about interrupting their husbands. But husbands and wives can both be positively bad-mannered at this point. We would never think of breaking in on a statement of a friend but do it with impunity with our spouse.

Let's eavesdrop on Phillip and June Pedemont. Phillip

loves to tell a funny story but, like so many of us, he has a limited repertoire. Those he knows, he tells fairly well, and to most of his listeners they sound pretty good, but not to June.

Phillip begins with, "Have you heard that story about the Baptist preacher who went to the circus . . ."

"Oh, Phillip, do you have to tell the old story again? It's got whiskers on it."

Phillip hesitates. He is thoroughly deflated. If he goes on it will be with a gnawing feeling of uncertainty and a grim suspicion that they have probably heard the tale a dozen times over. His wife, trying to save her friends, has effectively cut her husband down to size.

Who cares if June has heard the story twenty-five times over? Some musicians play a piece of music a hundred times, and the critics feel they do it better because of their practice. And, besides all this, Phillip was not really telling the story for June.

It is sometimes claimed that the pattern of German family life was set by Martin Luther, the monk who married a nun. Their marriage relationship was an open book. A horde of student boarders filled the large house, and many of them kept a record of every event in the reformer's life.

Among their recollections are found numerous examples of the way Martin and Katherine communicated with each other.

On one occasion as they sat eating their meal, Martin, in answer to a student's question, launched into a lengthy response. His wife Katherine sat with a mounting concern about the meal she had so carefully prepared, which was now becoming cold and unappetizing.

At last she could stand it no longer and said, "Doctor, why don't you stop talking and eat?"

The exasperated husband replied, "I wish that women would repeat the Lord's Prayer before opening their mouths."[2]

Martin himself was not above interrupting. In one petulant moment he interjected a sarcastic comment about her prayer. Katie was praying aloud for rain. Luther broke in, "Yes, why not, Lord? We have persecuted thy Word and killed thy saints. We have deserved well of thee."[3]

Yet we know from all the information on Luther's life that he loved Katherine very deeply. There were moments, however, when he felt the exasperation of his marriage relationship.

The Third Party

One of the most predictable features of a deteriorating marriage relationship is the attraction of either husband or wife to a third party. The really surprising aspect of these situations is the type of person to whom the erring husband or wife turns. In the language of some counselors, it is more likely to be a descending than an ascending infatuation.

Jim Heffner is a capable and successful businessman. Apparently happily married, he has an attractive wife and two lovely children. His wife Jean takes the situation for granted and is vaguely aware that she has a very satisfactory marriage. She speaks openly to her friends about the reliability of "dear old Jim."

The day comes when Mrs. Heffner is shocked beyond words. She accidently discovers her husband is having an "affair."

Further investigation shows his partner is neat, nicely dressed, not nearly as attractive as Jean, and certainly no glamorous sex pot. And she does not look like a seducer of married men.

When the showdown comes, Mrs. Heffner, after a period of blaming everything on her husband and "that woman," finally begins to ask herself where she has failed.

In answer to an inquiry as to what the other woman had that she lacked, Jim, her husband, replied, "She was genuinely interested in me. She sat and listened to what I had to say and tell."

Mrs. Heffner was mollified and was finally able to see that she was far too preoccupied with the children, P.T.A., her clubs, and a whole host of interests which kept her from taking much notice of her husband and his work. Above everything else she had failed in the perfectly simple technique of listening.

Communicating means giving the other person time to speak. I visited a radio ham who had established contact with a boyhood friend of mine. Now separated by about ten thousand miles, it was a thrill to hear his voice. I soon discovered there were no opportunities for interruption. When my friend in far off Australia had finished talking he turned the radio channel over to me, and not until then could I speak.

A good listener must always give the other person time. There must come a moment when, like the radio operator, he says, "Over to you." Only then will an adequate communication take place.

If there is to be a rewarding marriage relationship there must be adequate communication. Try these steps in re-establishing the communication process.

- Acknowledge the importance of communication and what it means in a marriage.
- Face the fact that *lack of listening* is probably the greatest point of failure in most marriages.
- Settle on a time when you are going to set aside a specific

period to listen to each other. Perhaps it could be Thursday night from 7 P.M. to 7:45 P.M.
- Arrange for a place where there are no children, no television, and a minimum possibility of interruption.
- If the situation is sensitive make a division of time: ten minutes for her, ten for him, the rest of the time for exchange.
- Agree there will be no interrupting, no flying off the handle, no sulking.

Following the ever popular "psychiatrist" theme, the cartoon showed a woman lying on the couch in the doctor's office. She was saying to the politely interested psychiatrist, "If only my husband would listen to me like you do!" And if he only would, it would save him a lot of time and give him a much more rewarding marriage.

CHAPTER 15

Dialogue and Self-Discovery

~~~~~~

Helen Keller was born a normal child. Nineteen months later, overtaken by a mysterious illness, she lingered at death's door, then suddenly and unaccountably recovered. To her parents' dismay they discovered the illness had left her deaf and blind, and, because of her deafness, she was mute.

Helen became, in her own words, ". . . a Phantom living in a world that was no-world."[1] She describes herself, "wild, unruly, giggling and chuckling to express pleasure; kicking, scratching, uttering the choked screams of the deaf mute to indicate the opposite."[2] She was condemned to stay in this "no-world" for five years.

Taken by her father to visit the famous inventor of the telephone, Dr. Alexander Graham Bell, he was advised to contact the Perkins Institution for the Blind in Boston. The visit started the monumental relationship with Anne Sullivan.

When Anne Sullivan began to work with Helen there was little response. Helen explains, "Alas, the Phantom had no sense of 'natural' bonds with humanity."[3]

Anne Sullivan soon discovered the kindly-disposed parents had been so permissive that the little blind girl was a law unto herself. Conscious of her privileged position, she exercised tyrannical reign over the household.

Speaking of herself in the third person, Helen recounts the battle of wills. "I remember her as plump, strong, reckless, and unafraid. She refused to be led, and had to be carried by force upstairs when she received her first lesson. Another time her table manners required correction. Phantom was in the habit of picking food out of her own plate and the plates of others with her fingers. Annie Sullivan would not put up with such behavior, and a fight followed during which the family left the room. Phantom acted like a demon, kicking, screaming, pinching her would-be deliverer and almost throwing her out of her chair, but Annie succeeded in compelling her to eat with a spoon and keep her hands out of the plate. Then Phantom threw her napkin on the floor, and after an hour's battle Annie made her pick it up and fold it. One morning Phantom would not sit down to learn words which meant nothing to her, and kicked over the table. When Annie put the table back in its place and insisted upon continuing the lesson, Phantom's fist flew like lightning and knocked out two of Annie's teeth."[4]

Realizing the indulgent parents would hinder the process of the education, Anne obtained their permission to take Helen off to Ivy Green, the vine-covered annex near the main house. In this totally new environment Anne literally wrestled with her ferocious little animal-child.

As Helen herself points out, in her "no-world" she was oblivious to time. Moreover, she had no sense of right or wrong. Never having lived in a knowledge of community with others, punishment just didn't mean anything.

Similarly, love was unappreciated. As Helen states it, "All the sweetness of childhood created by friendly voices and the light of smiling faces was dormant in her."[5]

After a frustrating month, and on the day earlier marked by a ferocious outburst of temper, there finally came the moment of breakthrough. Down at the well, redolent with the smell of the honeysuckle, the ever diligent teacher placed one of the little blind girl's hands under the flowing, icy cold water. All the while she ceaselessly spelt out the word "water" into her other hand. Then for Helen, in her own words, ". . . somehow the mystery of language was revealed to me. I knew then that 'w-a-t-e-r' meant the wonderful cool something that was flowing over my hand."[6]

Helen Keller, looking back on this event, called it ". . . my soul's sudden awakening."[7] It was obviously that, and more.

Helen's awakening came with the breakdown of the barriers of isolation which had cut her off from her fellows. The process of socialization was really under way. On the very day of Helen's "soul's sudden awakening" she had diverted her teacher's persistent efforts by seizing her new doll and hurling it to the floor.

Returning to the house from the pump, the memory of the morning returned to Helen. "On entering the door I remembered the doll I had broken. I felt my way to the hearth and picked up the pieces. I vainly tried to put them together. Then my eyes filled with tears; for I realized what I had done, and for the first time I felt repentance and sorrow."[8]

The Socializing Process

There is a peculiar sense in which every individual is born into the world alone, and a whole process generally referred to as socialization gets under way at the moment of birth. Easily the most important aspect of this experience is learning to communicate with and understand the world in which he has now come to live. This is done primarily by establishing "word linkages" with other people. It has been well stated, "Speech, again, is that through which we most commonly seek to escape our skin-enclosed isolation and to enter into a community of experience."[9]

In this episode of Helen Keller's life three aspects of socialization vividly stand out.

(1) Whereas much of the theorizing about human personality has focussed on the inner psychic life of the individual and the interactions of the systems, id, ego, and superego, it becomes increasingly obvious that attention must be paid to the social aspects of human experience.

From this perspective personality has been described by Harry Stack Sullivan as "the relatively enduring pattern of recurrent interpersonal situations which characterize a human life."[10] Proponents of this theory claim that even a hermit lives in the memory of the earlier relationships in which he was involved. To participate in these interpersonal situations it is necessary for the individual both to speak and to listen.

Entering into a sense of community with her fellows opened a pathway for Phantom to become Helen Keller— teacher, author, benefactress, and continuing inspirer of the handicapped.

(2) Much of the discussion of love, even apart from many of the romanticized notions, has centered on the importance of receiving love. Some studies have shown the dire effects of children growing up without love, which is said to be the one essential ingredient for achieving our humanity.

While there can be no doubt about the danger, particularly to those children that are institutionalized, to children deprived of love, it is easy to oversimplify the situation and overlook the giving aspect of love.

Helen received love. Her parents lavished affection upon her in such a prodigal manner that she became a virtual dictator in the Keller household. Instead of helping, the parents' loving permissiveness became the chief obstacle to Helen's achieving her personhood.

Anne Sullivan's work with Helen began with a demand for responsibility. The love of the dedicated teacher insisted that Helen learn obligations and the importance of giving to others.

Love may be thought of as a complex concept which involves at least three constituent elements: *eros* or selfish love, *Philia* or companionate love, and *agape* or giving love. Each of these elements in the triad is important. Any tendency to see love just as receiving, or even as sharing, as much superior as that is, will leave us with a deficient experience. Love at its best has to have the altruistic or giving element.

Much of the confusion of our modern ideas of love stems from a romantic, unreal expectation that love is something we get rather than something we give. Many marital difficulties arise from the strange egotistical and selfish anticipations with which many people enter marriage.

It seems to be particularly significant that as Helen was able to leave her "no-world" and enter the world of reality she became less selfish and increasingly idealistic as she gave herself in service for her fellows.

(3) Leaving the "no-world" to enter the real world brought a sense of values to Helen. If conscience is ". . . the internalized voice of an idealized society," it follows that the closer our contact with society, the more sensitive will our conscience be.

Prior to her experience at the well, Helen had no respect for the rights of others. She had to be forcibly carried to her lesson; her table manners were appalling as she refused to use a spoon and with her fingers took food from the plates of others. She kicked over the table, refused to fold her napkin, and during the scuffle knocked out two of her teacher's teeth.

At the pump came contact with Anne Sullivan and the society she represented. One of the first results was a sense of obligation and failure. She remembered the broken doll and for the first time was conscious of repentance and sorrow as she tried to repair the damage.

Meaningful living never takes place in isolation. As we become aware of society's expectations and learn to live within its boundaries, we increasingly realize the possibilities of healthy living. Our capacity for the inward discomfort we call guilt is itself an indication of meaningful living.

When the dedicated teacher made contact with Helen's incarcerated spirit she opened a channel which allowed the release of the imprisoned splendor. Step by step Helen Keller moved forward to college, fame, and a lifetime of service to her fellows.

All of this was achieved because there was a concerned person who helped her establish contact and realize her potential.

CHAPTER 16

Confession—
Into the Arms of Humanity

~~~~~~

No greater evidence exists to show the need of most people for a listening ear than the growth of interest in the time-honored practice of confession. While some of this has come within some churches, the most dramatic upsurge has taken place in a wide variety of organizations which have discovered the values of confession in helping troubled people in such diverse areas as alcoholism, drug addiction, obesity, and mental illness.

All forms of religion have a place for confession. In the Old Testament a disobedient Achan was called upon to confess his failure before the assembled children of Israel. Levitical priests exhorted the Israelites to confess their iniquities. Solomon, the wisest of all kings, reminded his readers, "He that covereth his sins shall not prosper but whoso confesseth and forsaketh them shall have mercy."[1] The psalmist in his personal upset and turmoil came to the realization that confession brought relief and a feeling of well-being.

The New Testament continues the emphasis. James urges the Christians to "confess your faults one to another."[2] The practice was carried over into the primitive church. When a believer had failed to live by the standards of his Christian profession he told the whole church group of his failure. They in turn practiced church discipline, laying some special obligation on the erring member.

In the change of emphasis which came over the church in about the fourth century, confession underwent a subtle but debilitating change. Some historians refer to the process as "the sealing of the confessional." The main change was that confession was no longer made to the whole church but to one individual under a cloak of secrecy.

With the rise of the Reformation Movement many practices of the Roman Church came under attack. Interestingly enough, the reformer Martin Luther was not so sure as to whether confession should be excluded from church practices. Bainton says of Luther, "He looked upon confession as useful, provided it was not institutionalized."[3] Nevertheless, the suspicion of priestly practices was so strong that confession gradually disappeared in Protestantism as emphasis was laid on confession to God alone without the help of any earthly mediator.

Confessional techniques came to be either formalized and deadened by ecclesiastical legalism as in Roman Catholicism, or downgraded and disowned as by the Protestants. Such was the need for a listening ear that even as the church cast aside this powerful technique there were others waiting to pick it up and exploit it.

In the new scientific surge of the nineteenth century came the formulation of theories and laws about the mind and mental functionings. While this theorizing used the language of science, in actual practice, the techniques were old, for at the heart of it all was the experience of confession.

In the forefront of the new movement were men like Sigmund Freud, Alfred Adler, and C. J. Jung. Although they were schooled in the medical practices of their day, they nevertheless brought news of nonphysical ways to assist people whose malfunctioning minds brought them far greater problems than had bodily disorders. Despite all the new language, as Jung himself noted, psychoanalysis was really development of "its prototype, the confessional."[4] The psychiatrist is careful to disavow any causal relationship but sees psychoanalysis as taking up the long-known confessional technique as a means of helping people.

Jung's theorizing was particularly interesting. He claimed that man's troubles came upon him because of the secrets he kept within the inner sanctum of his personality. So he says, "As soon as man was capable of conceiving the idea of sin, he had recourse to psychic concealment—or, to put it in analytical language, repressions arose. Anything that is concealed is a secret. The maintenance of secrets acts like a psychic poison which alienates their possessor from the community."[5] The experience so carefully hidden can be kept a secret even from ourselves. This secret he sees as having a separate existence in the unconscious.

The answer to all this is seen by the psychotherapist to lie in some technique which would reverse the process of secrecy that brought on the difficulty. It is by confession that the perplexed sufferer finds his way back to community and well-being.

The New, Old Confession

The practice of confession periodically reappears among groups of people seeking to help their fellows. In the early days of the Wesleyan revival the Methodist Church had its class meetings in which the people were divided by age and sex into groups. The leader stood to tell of his spiritual condition and failures, then invited the other members to relate their own experiences.

Later came the Oxford Group with its emphasis on "sharing" before the group. From this group two men went out to form the highly influential Alcoholics Anonymous. At the heart of their technique stands their Twelve Steps with two pivotal statements: "Made a searching and fearless moral inventory of ourselves" and "Admitted to God and to another human being the exact nature of our wrongs."[6] Personal responsibility followed by openness occupies a central place in the method which has had tremendous success with alcoholics.

In the same line of succession stands Integrity Therapy, a new technique for helping people in difficulty. It lays a heavy emphasis on confession, but in its theorizing emphasizes three distinctives which make the confessional experience unique.

In most of the systems of psychotherapy the primary aim of any type of confession is "catharsis," "abreaction," or "ventilation," which allows the expression of emotion. Integrity Therapy subjects may give expression to their emotion, an experience which is respected by the group. But this is not seen as a primary purpose nor is it necessarily of any great value by itself.

A second difference is that Integrity Therapy insists confession must lead to appropriate activity or behavior. Confession is never an end in itself.

The third distinctive concerns the question, "To whom should I confess?" In most systems of religion and psychotherapy the recipient of the confession is one particular person—priest, therapist, analyst, or counselor. This is a thoroughly trained individual, very conscious of his role, who generally warns the "counselee" or "patient" against further confession to anyone else. There seem to be vague warnings of the possible damage arising from such indiscreet activity, and the therapeutic role of the group is overlooked.

Integrity Therapy rejects the notion of just one special person to whom confession should be made under the cloak of secrecy. An experience like this may only create another secret. The subject has been putting on a false front to his fellows and now has the need to disclose himself to others. This is not an advocacy of indiscriminate confession but calls for confession either to those whom he has deceived or people who are representative of, or symbolize them. A therapy group provides this background against which the exploration of self takes place.

The Fine Art of Confession

The word "confession" has been used in many different ways, and, to help clear the air, Integrity Therapy has laid down some guidelines that help to elucidate the nature of legitimate and therapeutic confession.

- Confession is not complaining.
- Confession is not blaming others for our problems and difficulties.
- We do not confess for others but concentrate on our own shortcomings.
- Confession focuses on our faults and failures rather than our strengths.
- Confession is never made indiscriminately, but rather to "significant others" in our lives.
- Confession is a willingness to come under the judgment of our fellows.

The age-old practice of confession is coming into its own again and in the most unlikely situations. There are many applications of a time-honored principle. As Jung says with a fine turn of phrase, "In keeping the matter private . . . I still continue in my state of isolation. It is only with the help of confession that I am able to throw myself into the arms of humanity freed at last from the burden of moral exile."[7] And the one indispensable person in a confessional is a listener.

CHAPTER 17

The Heart
of the Counseling Process

From the crowded room of adults came the babble of animated conversation. On the outer fringe of a tight group wandered the small boy, whose whole demeanor shouted that he was feeling left out and lonely. By way of contrast, the little fellow's father was in the heart of it all, and the circle gathered around him participated in an excited verbal interchange.

Edging through the crowd, the small boy finally made it to his father's side where he stood trying to attract his daddy's attention by gently tugging his pants' leg.

The father warmed to the discussion. It was obviously his moment. Only vaguely aware of his offspring, he had no desire to slow down or interrupt his presentation. But the boy was not to be ignored. He persisted with an occasional plaintive, "Daddy ... Daddy ..."

Reluctantly turning from his friends, the father excused himself and gave the boy his total attention. "Yes, son, what is it?"

The child stood in awed silence. He was either overwhelmed by the sudden attention, or had forgotten what he intended to say.

Modern man is in a similar predicament. An automated

atomic age has become increasingly depersonalized, leaving him lonely, bewildered, and wondering if he really counts. The very successes of the physical sciences in constructing computers and complex automated machines have complicated the task of the social scientist. And after all his carefully planned research and investigation, the psychotherapist frequently returns to the simplest and most effective technique of all for helping troubled people—listening.

As a student in Paris working with Dr. Breuer, the youthful Sigmund Freud learned of an event which had left an indelible impression on his teacher's mind. While using hypnosis in psychotherapy Dr. Breuer had been surprised by a woman patient who said, "Dr. Breuer, if you would allow me to talk to you and tell you how my symptoms started, I think it would help me."[1] Breuer let her talk, and after she had verbalized her troubles the psychotherapist noted a perceptible improvement. They came to refer to the technique as "the talk cure."

In the growth of his own distinctive system of psychotherapy Freud came to believe most people were in difficulty because of repressed material deeply buried in the submerged and shadowy unconscious. Because this area of the mind was beyond the field of awareness it was almost impossible for the sufferer to discover and work through these repressions. As a means of getting at the elusive unconscious, Freud adapted the "talk cure" and gave it a central place in his therapy.

The patient lay on a couch and talked on in a freewheeling stream of conversation while the psychoanalyst sat at his head, listened, and considered all that was said. The therapist later endeavored to interpret the ideas expressed by his subject. The technique came to be known as "free association."

Sigmund Freud was destined to leave the stamp of his life and work on the whole field of the behavioral sciences. His theorizing was frequently complex, not a little poetic, but attractive to workers in psychology, psychiatry, social work, and education. Many followers in these fields became enamored with his poetic speculation, developmental explanation, psychic determinism, and overlooked the simple lesson he had unconsciously taught—that many people badly need someone to listen to them.

Among those influenced by Freudian theory there sprang into existence a whole group of psychotherapeutic techniques known as the "expressive therapies." Some of these showed considerable ingenuity. People were put onto a stage in psychodrama; given canvas, palette and paint in art therapy; encouraged to participate in games in play therapy; placed in an audience to witness the dramatic performance of tiny figures in puppet therapy. All these procedures aimed at providing experiences that would help distressed people find some type of expression.

Another theorist was near at hand to place the listening technique in a new and much simpler system of psychotherapy. Carl Rogers, with an optimism about human nature that had previously characterized the progressive education movement, insisted that most human beings had a drive towards mental health and adjustment. To set them free it was mainly the task of the counselor to devise simple ways of encouraging them to talk.

The adroitness of the nondirective therapist lay in not interrupting or slowing down the verbalizing of the counselee. Simple reflective statements helped the concerned person continue to talk as he expressed and dissipated the emotion which had built up blockages and immobilized the client's intellectual capacities.

The really skillful client-centered therapist spent long hours learning to encourage the subject to verbalize. Thus he became the listener par excellence.

Rogerian theory's objective was insight for the counselee. The distinctive Rogerian view of insight involved three ideas: the perception of relationships, the acceptance of self, and the element of choice. To reach this goal Rogers tells those who are anxious to learn some new revolutionary technique, "The answer is bound to be a disappointing one to the over eager . . . . The primary technique is to encourage the expression of attitudes and feelings . . . until insightful understanding appears spontaneously."[2] Listening is the "open sesame" to the neurotic's prison house.

Even in the more directive systems of counseling there is always some distinctive place for listening. I once worked with Dr. O. Hobart Mowrer, the originator of Integrity Therapy. On the platform Mowrer is forthright and aggressive, but sitting with him in initial interviews and therapy sessions I could not help but note how unusually gentle he was with troubled people. Although he bore in and insisted people face their personal irresponsibilities, he also spent long periods of time patiently listening to the story the counselee had to tell.

Within Integrity Therapy groups there is also an insistence on responsibility and openness. Group members will frequently challenge the contributor and zero in with a demand that he cease blaming his background, other people, or the circumstances of life. Yet after long, long hours in group work, the abiding memory remains of a counselee's telling his story while eight or nine people in the group hang on every word. Listening is a vital part of this activity.

The Listener

John Godfrey, after a life of professional mediocrity, finally retired from his practice of law. He was a widower, his wife having died years before. He had taken the loss with such fortitude that some thought he must not have had a great deal of love for her. His interests in life were few and he was not widely known.

At eighty years of age Godfrey launched himself upon an unusual project. It was done in secrecy and, when completed, caused a sensation in the city where he lived.

Taylor Caldwell, who writes of Godfrey in her book *The Listener,* says it was the day after his eightieth birthday that he consulted the puzzled architects about a new building to be erected upon the piece of land where his clapboard house had stood for so long.

After much speculation the townspeople were astonished to see a beautiful marble building take shape. Some thought that it might be a church, but they were wrong. Surrounded by attractive gardens with red gravel paths, it was square in shape and contained just two rooms. The massive bronze doors were inscribed in gold letters with the words, "The Man Who Listens."

The entrance led to a waiting room. Here the visitors sat until their turn to enter the inner room through the oaken door. Inside the room a single chair faced an arched alcove hidden by the blue curtains. Alongside was the inscription: "If you wish to see the man who has listened to you, touch the button above. You will see his face. He will be glad if you thank him, but it is not necessary."[3]

John Godfrey offered an explanation as to why he had provided the building and its unusual facilities: "One of the most terrible aspects of this world today is that nobody listens to anyone else. If you are sick, or even dying, nobody listens. If you are bewildered, or frightened, or lost, or be-reaved, or alone, or lonely—nobody listens. Even the clergy are hurried and harassed; they do their best and work end-lessly. But time has taken on a fragmented character; it doesn't seem to have any substance any longer. Nobody has time to listen to anyone, not even those who love you and would die for you. Your parents, your children, your friends: they have not the time. That's a very terrible thing, isn't it? Whose fault is it? I don't know. But there doesn't seem to be any time."[4]

So Godfrey had made possible a constantly available listen-ing ear.

The remaining chapters of Miss Caldwell's book are given to telling a whole series of modern parables depicting the dilemma of people who need someone to listen to them.

The underprivileged factory worker comes to complain about his wife and family and lot in life. A Negro who wants to be a minister of the gospel laments that he cannot do any better than work as a cook and dishwasher. The prosperous businessman relates his story of a crooked partner. A Jewish father tells the tale of his struggle to educate the doctor son who now has cancer. An unwed mother wrestles with her decision to marry a respectable farmer who is willing to forget the past. The successful but distraught clergyman bares his soul before the blue cur-tains. And so on and on, moving through the procession, come doctor, judge, architect, scientist, to tell of their prob-lems.

The story makes interesting reading for a psychologist, as it tells many of the experiences which are frequently heard in the consulting room. The impression that strikes the most responsive chord is the flow of the interviews. The listener never says a word, not even an "eloquent grunt." Yet in

each instance the person who comes to talk discovers a hitherto unnoticed aspect of his problems and a new direction
in which to turn.

Tab Shutts enters the listener's room to complain about
the inequities of life and bewail the fact that he never had a
chance. Kept out of school to help support the family, with
no training or preparation, he wanders from one dead-end
job to another. Army service brings temptation, sin, and frustration. His forced marriage leads to contention and cruelty.
He refers to his spouse: "Fran—she's my wife, she's the one
with the jeans and the lipstick and the big fat can—."[5]

The ambitious wife, forever complaining and pushing,
tries to maneuver him into a place for advancement. Everything she does is wrong in Tab's eyes. Whining on, he com-
plains, laments, and grouches. At last his interminable recital
takes a reflective turn, "Come to think of it, women don't
have such a hot time, do they? They get pretty, then they
marry...."

The frustrated, self-pitying complainer pauses, thinks in
silence for a while and adds softly, "And then they marry
jerks like me. That's what they do. They marry jerks like
me."[6]

So a measure of self-understanding came to Tab Shutts
when a listening ear was available to him.

While it is highly improbable that such a device would
really work, the novelist with her literary licence has drama-
tized a psychological truth. When we verbalize our thoughts,
when we put them into words and so externalize them, we
are able to look at them from a new perspective. And it is
the listener who helps us do this.

The Test of Verbalization

At a gathering of psychiatrists and ministers, a speaker

discussed the reasons for the gathering and in a perceptive summation asked the question, "How can I know what I think until I hear myself say it?" He was obviously saying he needed someone to listen to him to be able to come to a better self-understanding.

Mental processes can be deceptive, for the human mind has the capacity to think unreal thoughts. This distinctly human ability to engage in fantasy has meant a heightening of his potential. Unhampered by his lack of experience, he can imagine possibilities, and from his daydreams may emerge new and creative activity. But the borderline between creative imagination and pathological fantasy is very narrow. In one instance it may lead to creative enterprise, in the other to the shadowy world of hallucination and delusion.

Men need to test their thoughts. The inner world of ideas must be exteriorized and examined to discover if they will stand up in the world of reality. One of the best ways of doing this is by the "test of verbalization." The simple process of expressing ideas helps to clarify them. While working on writing a book I have discovered it needs revision after I have used it as lecture material in my classes. Hearing myself verbalize the ideas, I am able to evaluate them more critically.

Niebuhr speaks about "The Internal Dialogue of Self" and notes that man is probably the only animal with a need to talk to himself. It might be imagined he could best do this by sitting in a corner and thinking furiously. Experience has shown, however, that this is best done by speaking to others. Any lecturer has two audiences, the people sitting in front of him and *himself*. As we listen to him we frequently allow him to say something to himself.

Psychotherapy is probably at its worst when it has become

dependent upon physical and chemical techniques. Whatever temporary alleviation of symptoms they may bring, the
use of insulin therapy, electro-shock, and tranquilizers have
frequently had disappointing sequels.

Dominick Barbara, the psychoanalyst, presents another
possibility: "The psychotherapist's most important tool is
listening."[7] In her *Principles of Intensive Psychotherapy*, the
great authority Dr. Frieda Fromm-Reichmann says: "What
then are the basic requirements as to the personality and
professional abilities of the psychiatrist? If I were asked to
answer this question in one sentence, I would reply, 'The
psychotherapist must be able to listen.' "[8]

Listening is the primary counseling method.

CHAPTER 18

The Listener's Finest Hour

Mrs. Newkirk, thirty-five years old and the fond mother of twin girls, was popular with her friends and apparently accepting the normal responsibilities of life. Her husband had achieved in his vocation and they owned a nice home in a middle-class area of the city.

Then her world tumbled in. After a few spells of anxiety she sank into a deep depression. Life looked bleak to her. Everything was wrong. Sitting languidly in her chair, she sighed deeply and could see no future for herself. It just didn't seem to be worth it all.

Friends, relatives, and neighbors speculated as to what had happened to their once cheerful neighbor. Some of the women vaguely hinted it was probably related to her "time in life," which had arrived prematurely. Her mother recalled a time when as a girl she had fallen from a window and hit herself on the head. There were questions about her childhood asked by others. Some thought it might have been the strain of her term as P.T.A. program chairman.

There is another possibility.

She may not have listened! ! !

She may not have listened to *herself*. She had listened to the children, in part at least to the minister's sermon on Sunday, occasionally to her husband, to television and radio programs, to her friends and a thousand other voices; but she had overlooked a voice within.

Each of us has a conscience sometimes called "the internalized voice of an idealized society." Some psychologists call this the Superego, meaning "greater I," which is a representative of the values we hold even though they be unconscious.

The executive system of personality is the Ego or I, the decision-making self. When the decisions of the Ego (I) are not in harmony with the Superego (greater I) we are driven to hiding our deviant activity.

A man took an unwanted cat out into the countryside in an effort to lose it. He turned it loose and returned with a feeling of confidence that that would be the last of it all. A few nights later he was awakened by a plaintive meow of the cat at the back door. In a similar manner the unwanted experiences of life may return to haunt us.

Mrs. Newkirk's depression may have been a symptom. Belgum has described symptoms as "the amplified and distorted voice of conscience." When we fail to listen to the "still small voice of conscience" it manifests itself in symptoms like depression, anxiety, sleeplessness, or some type of functional illness.

While many of us are concerned about the God who spoke in creation and declared His demands of men in the thunder of Mount Sinai, we frequently overlook the One who speaks through an inner voice. The story of Elijah's conflict with the prophets of Baal tells of the depression which followed his triumphant experience. God spoke to the prophet. First there was the lightning and the thunder but God was not in this manifestation of power. Then came the *still small voice*. This was the authentic voice of God.

It could be that many of us are forever talking because we do not want to listen, not just to others but to ourselves. If we are silent we may hear a voice which tells us of our inner failure. Niebuhr refers to the "Internal Dialogue of Self." Listening to the inner voice, we can discover ourselves.

There is one continuing theme running through the Bible. It is that men must *listen* if they are to know God. The all important commandment said by Jesus to be the "first and the greatest" commences with "Hear, O Israel." Many times over Jesus warned His followers, "He that hath ears to hear, let him hear," and Paul reminds us "faith cometh by hearing."

When Glenn Clark interviewed the noted Negro scientist George Washington Carver he asked what was the secret of his success in discovering so many of the secrets of nature. The scientist replied, ". . . all my life I have risen at four o'clock and have gone into the woods and talked with God. There He gives me my orders for the day. . . . When people are still asleep I hear God best and learn my plan."

If we will really seek to know and listen for the voice of God, then we may have the experience of one of a bygone day of whom it was said, "And thine ear shall hear a voice behind thee, saying, 'This is the way, walk ye in it.'"

If we hear this voice we are blessed indeed.

REFERENCES

~~~~~~

CHAPTER ONE

1. Taylor Caldwell, *The Listener* (New York: Doubleday and Company, Inc., 1920), Foreword.

CHAPTER TWO

1. Whittaker Chambers, *Witness* (New York: Random House, 1952), p. 16.

CHAPTER THREE

1. Helmut Thielicke, *Encounter With Spurgeon* (Philadelphia: Fortress Press, 1963), p. 236-37.

2. *Ibid.*, p. 235.

3. Ralph G. Nichols and Leonard A. Stevens, *Are You Listening?* (New York: McGraw-Hill Book Company, Inc., 1957), p. 34.

CHAPTER FOUR

1. John W. Drakeford, *Integrity Therapy—A New Direction in Psychotherapy* (Nashville, Tenn.: Broadman Press, 1967).

CHAPTER FIVE

1. E. D. Fales, Jr., "Can You Talk to Other Drivers?" *Reader's Digest*, LXXVII (May, 1966), 177.

2. *Ibid.*, p. 180.

3. *Ibid.*

4. "Action in the Pits," *Time*, July 1, 1966, p. 73A.

5. A. B. Patterson, *The Collected Verse of A. B. Patterson* (Sydney: Angus and Robertson, Ltd., 1942), p. 45.

6. Beth Day, "Standing Room Only For Silence," *Reader's Digest*, LXXII (June, 1958), 187.

CHAPTER SIX

1. Paul Simon, "Sound of Silence," *The Best of Simon and Garfunkel* (New York: Electric Music Company), p. 3.
2. Theodor Reik, *Listening With The Third Ear* (New York: Grove Press, Inc., 1948), p. 126.
3. Anne Morrow Lindbergh, *Gift From the Sea* (New York: Pantheon Books, Random House, Inc., 1955), pp. 115-16.

CHAPTER SEVEN

1. Norman R. Jaffray, "Good Listener," *Saturday Evening Post*, CCXXXL (December 6, 1958), 40.

CHAPTER NINE

1. Nichols and Stevens, p. 53.

CHAPTER TEN

1. Nardi Reeder Campion, "Ask, Don't Tell," *Reader's Digest*, LXXXIX (August, 1966), 51.
2. *Ibid.*, pp. 51-52.
3. *Ibid.*, p. 50.

CHAPTER TWELVE

1. Campion, p. 50.
2. Nehemiah Curnock (ed.), *The Journal of Reverend John Wesley, M.A.* (London: The Epworth Press, 1909), I, 291-92.
3. Horace B. English and Ava Champney English, *A Comprehensive Dictionary of Psychological and Psychoanalytical Terms* (New York: Longmans Green & Company, 1958), p. 437.
4. Dale Carnegie, *How to Win Friends and Influence People* (New York: Simon and Schuster, 1937), p. 115.

CHAPTER THIRTEEN

1. Isaac Deutscher, *Stalin* (New York: Vintage Books, 1960), p. 274.
2. *Ibid.*, pp. 250-51.
3. *Ibid.*, p. 248.
4. *Ibid.*, p. 274.
5. Norman Rockwell, "My Adventures as an Illustrator," ed. T. Rockwell, *Saturday Evening Post*, CCXXXII (April 2, 1960), 67.
6. Frank Freidel, "America Enters The Modern Era," *National Geographic*, CXXVIII (October, 1965), 570.
7. Nichols and Stevens, *Are You Listening?* p. 36.
8. Dominick A. Barbara, *The Art of Listening* (Springfield: Charles C Thomas, 1958), p. 56.
9. Stewart Alsop, "The Face of the President-1966," *Saturday Evening Post*, CCXXXIX (September 24, 1966), 24.
10. Nichols and Stevens, pp. 160-1.

CHAPTER FOURTEEN

1. Marjorie Holmes, "Why Men Don't Talk to Their Wives," *Today's Health*, XXXVI (August, 1958), 38.
2. Roland Bainton, *Here I Stand* (Nashville: Abingdon Press, 1950), p. 301.
3. *Ibid.*

CHAPTER FIFTEEN

1. Helen Keller, *Teacher: Anne Sullivan Macy* (Garden City, New York: Doubleday Company, Inc., 1955), p. 8.
2. *The World Book Encyclopedia* (Chicago: Field Enterprises Educational Corporation, 1964), II, 209.
3. Helen Keller, *Teacher*, p. 37.
4. *Ibid.*, p. 38.
5. *Ibid.*, p. 37.
6. Helen Keller, *The Story of My Life* (New York: Doubleday, Doran and Company, Inc., 1933), p. 23.
7. *Ibid.*, p. 25.
8. *Ibid.*, p. 24.
9. H. A. Overstreet, *The Mature Mind* (New York: W. W. Norton Company, Inc., 1949), pp. 54-57.
10. Calvin S. Hall and Gardiner Lindzey, *Theories of Personality* (New York: John Wiley and Sons, Inc., 1950), p. 134.

CHAPTER SIXTEEN

1. Proverbs 28:13.
2. James 5:16.
3. Bainton, p. 137.
4. C. G. Jung, *Modern Man in Search of a Soul* (New York: Harcourt Brace & Company, 1933), p. 31.
5. *Ibid.*
6. *Alcoholics Anonymous* (New York: Alcoholics Anonymous Publishing, Inc., 1955), p. 59.
7. Jung, p. 35.

CHAPTER SEVENTEEN

1. A. A. Brill, *Fundamental Conceptions of Psychoanalysis* (New York: Harcourt, Brace and Company, Inc., 1921), p. 7.
2. Carl R. Rogers, *Counseling and Psychotherapy* (Cambridge: Houghton Mifflin, 1942), p. 195.
3. Taylor Caldwell, *The Listener* (New York: Doubleday and Company, Inc., 1960), p. 20.
4. *Ibid.*, p. 21.
5. *Ibid.*, p. 43.
6. *Ibid.*, p. 47.
7. Barbara, p. 153.
8. Frieda Fromm-Reichman, *Principles of Intensive Psychotherapy* (Chicago: University of Chicago Press, 1950), p. 7.